A

20/20

VISION

A NEW

20/20

VISION

Cultivate Joy, Reprogram Your Mind,
and Define Life Through an Authentic Lens

By

TAYLOR ROCHESTIE

A New 20/20 Vision

Cultivate Joy, Reprogram Your Mind, and Define Life Through an Authentic Lens

Published by Wisdom House Books, Inc.
Chapel Hill, North Carolina 27516 USA
1.919.883.4669 | www.wisdomhousebooks.com

Wisdom House Books is committed to excellence in the publishing industry.

Book design copyright © 2021 by Wisdom House Books, Inc. All rights reserved.

Cover and Interior Design by Ted Ruybal
Edited by Jessie Davidson and Will Walton

Published in the United States of America

Paperback ISBN: 978-1-7359868-0-7
LCCN: 2020920651

SEL027000 | SELF-HELP / Personal Growth / Success
SEL040000 | SELF-HELP / Communication & Social Skills
SPO004000 | SPORTS & RECREATION / Basketball

First Edition

25 24 23 22 21 20 / 10 9 8 7 6 5 4 3 2 1

A BLESSING FOR JOY AND LÉON

I wish for you to have a full heart and a kind soul. I hope that your eyes give you vision through lenses of faith, not fear. I hope that your brightness is seen by everyone, and especially in the reflection you see in the mirror. Shine, even when the lights are off. The world is extremely complex—full of incredible potential and the optimistic unknown. Find your path through trials and many errors. Navigate your journey with strength and trust in yourself, and through the strong foundation of the relationships you build. Believe in the power of love. Spread inspiration and kindness to all people from all walks of life. Our power is that we are all the same because we are all uniquely different. Everyone deserves love, so always feel deserving. Stay humble throughout your journey. Be active in your happiness, every day.

TABLE OF CONTENTS

Acknowledgments...ix

Introduction...xi

    Chapter 1: Rooted in Happiness.........................1

    Chapter 2: Find Your Authentic Self....................7

    Chapter 3: Communication.............................17

    Chapter 4: Reprogramming the Mind...................69

    Chapter 5: Finding Daily Happiness..................131

    Chapter 6: Your Happiest You.......................165

    Chapter 7: Inspire Inspiration.....................175

Conclusion..183

Index..185

About the Author...187

ACKNOWLEDGMENTS

To my wife, Agathe—For opening my heart to see true beauty, inside and out. For accepting me in all my authenticity. For our family, for the power of love, and for creating a Home wherever life takes us. Ensemble Pour La Vie.

To my kids—For inspiring my words, and giving me redefined purpose and joy. For giving me a new vision, and helping me to see the world again through youthful eyes.

To my brother—For being my best friend since the day I was born. For inspiring my creativity and my imagination. For your support in all I do, and all the laughs along the way. For being my role model to this day.

Mama—Your loving spirit and unconditional love. For instilling in me a love for family, fun, and the importance of tradition. For inspiring me to create a meaningful life, filled with big dreams, hard work, curiosity and travel.

Pop—For highlighting the power of unconditional love and gratitude. For your optimism and courage to always choose happiness. For shaping my new 2020 vision.

Jessie—For turning my words into a story, and pages into a book. This is all possible, thanks to your ideas, vision, and thoughtfulness.

To my friends and family, acquaintances and strangers. I live in gratitude for everyone and everything around me.

INTRODUCTION

The Journey Begins:

2020 will be remembered.

2020 inspired the world to seek a new way of being. The year provided a crucial pause in life and presented us with a clear and imperative choice: be hopeful that an external solution will bring answers and normalcy back to our lives, or be proactive in creating a new reality by putting thoughts into action, actively designing an inspired vision for our future.

We will determine if 2020 was a time of unrest and uncertainty, or a time of liberation and actualization. The world was flipped upside down, and we can't just turn it back over and pick up where we left off. We must seize our moment, give purpose to our actions, and restructure the very nature in which our world operates.

I am a professional basketball player, having played for over eleven years in Europe and China. In March, 2020, the Covid-19 virus ended my season in Greece, months ahead of schedule. My wife,

Agathe, was to give birth to our son, Léon, in June. With airports closing, we took the last flight out of Greece to get to France, in order to be with Agathe's family for the birth. Upon arrival, quarantine isolated us from family and friends during this critical moment in our lives. The uncertainty that impacted my family was compounded by unrest on a global scale.

I remember looking into the eyes of my daughter, Joy, pondering the world she will inherit and wondering what kind of world Léon was being born into. Are we going to let the world define who we are and who we can become?

This is our life, our choice, and our time.

I have never been more optimistic about the present, never so hopeful for the world my children are living in, as I am today. My eyes are open, and I am ready to be part of the solution, part of building a brighter future, knowing that 2020 was the catalyst for positive change.

Are you ready to make changes?

ROOTED IN HAPPINESS

Fatherhood has expanded my world exponentially, and lately it seems like life has been moving faster than ever. When I became a father, I felt my eyes open wider, as if I was seeing the world through a new lens. Similar to my wedding day, happiness took priority in my vision of the world. These feelings of pure joy sparked my curiosity to know how happiness is experienced and created? Why is it difficult to access sometimes? Is there a way I can create happiness organically, and can it be passed down to the next generation?

Now, we are in a new decade, and it is challenging us and our happiness in ways we've never imagined. The 2020s find us with a heightened sense of individual identity but a struggle to actually identify it, constantly search for meaning. We look outward to align our identities through popular information and popular ideology. And what do we see when we look outside of ourselves? We see a society easily distracted by possessions—one waiting for validation from a world telling us what it means to be successful. Social media has increasing influence on our minds, defining the world we live in and what we consider to be important. External voices have led to a socially influenced state of mind and an inauthentic self-image.

We are more connected than ever before, yet we no longer prioritize what it means to be truly connected. The world has never been more accessible, yet it seems we're more unhappy and alone than past generations. More and more, young adults are speaking out about the depression, anxiety, and loneliness that they experience. While past generations may have dealt with many of the same feelings, we are at a new age of expressionism and openness about speaking our truths. A new social acceptance of what we are going through gives us the platform to explore these new emotions, yet doesn't always provide the answers to helping us sort through the complexity of our state of mind. We often look outward to help us accept who we are, and find answers to internally complex questions.

When society defines and influences our personal happiness, we're constrained by a narrow view that "this" or "that" will make us feel "happy" or "unhappy." To live like this is unsustainable and destructive. It's time to dig deep, find our purpose-filled voice, and redefine happiness on our own terms.

There are mornings when happiness comes more easily, like a child waking up on their birthday, anticipating a joy-filled day. Some mornings, however, are more challenging, fearing you'll face personal pain, suffering, or some seemingly insurmountable challenge. But, challenging days and happiness are not mutually exclusive.

Unhappiness is a mindset; it's a reactive feeling that is developed over time, through personal experiences, expectations, and projections. We measure our happiness by looking into the future or by comparing our present to our past, finding our distorted reality somewhere in the middle. If we had no memory of the past, and were unable to imagine the future, then unhappiness would have no reference point within our logic or understanding. I believe that, in order for us to experience unhappiness, our mind has to actively be distorted by external factors that cloud our reality.

Let's agree on one crucial idea: We're not born unhappy.

Unknowingly, we have adopted an unhealthy and unattainable hierarchy of importance, creating internal struggle to find, define, and sustain happiness. This struggle leads us to believe that we are unhappy—triggers from outside, set off in your mind, influence how you're feeling and your outlook on the day.

Our brains are not wired to be unhappy. Sure, we all have experienced some form of unhappiness, pain, or struggle in our lives. Some mornings when we wake up, we resign ourselves to the feeling of unhappiness, letting it transform our daily experience. We concede to the unhappiness and even accept its presence: "Well, that's life." Happiness is not found in the denial of unhappiness but rather in the acceptance and reprogramming of it. If we have the ability to experience unhappiness, we are just as capable of reprogramming our mind to organically create happiness as well.

Ask yourself: Is there a chance that your daily experiences could be approached in a way that would inspire happiness in your life? If you answered "yes," then you have an optimistic belief that happiness can, in fact, be a part of your everyday life.

The goal of this book is to provide a new framework for experiencing happiness. In order to choose our happiness, we first need to define it on a personal level, and then relearn where to look for it in our everyday lives. Let's find the triggers that control our moods and emotions. Let's dissect the hold social influence has on our happiness. Let's understand the importance of authentic communication and the significant role it plays in sustainable happiness.

It's time to take back ownership of our own life, control our own narrative, and define our own happiness and success. More than ever, we need a framework for how we prioritize our values and reconnect with one another.

I began my journey of writing this book by identifying 6 ways to create sustainable happiness:

- Understand who you are—from how you got here to where you want to go.

- Practice constant thankfulness. Being thankful doesn't actually require something to be thankful for.

- Communicate authentically to inspire and build relationships based on a true understanding of love, acceptance, and equality for all people.

- Reprogram your mind by finding a new lens through which to see the world.

- Develop and nurture your happiness through daily applications.

- Inspire others.

These are the truths that give structure to how I engage in life—the choices I make and the way I support those around me each and every day.

Happiness—what an incredible concept. It is not just a feeling; it's a limitless, complex, yet accessible, emotion. Happiness has an exponential capacity for growth. It is not just a reaction to an experience or interaction; it's a passion and skill you can develop and nurture over time. Happiness is attainable for all people. Know that you deserve happiness, and that you must take control and be active in its creation every day.

To some, happiness or unhappiness is measured by going through a checklist of perceived criteria based on personal or social pressure. House? Yes. Job? No. Friends? Yes. Partner? No. To some, happiness can be disguised in the form of a "like" or "mention" on social media. It can be temporarily felt in the applause from a crowd or a pat on the back for a job well done. Some of us feel happy each time we get our paycheck, or in the recognition of our work and accomplishments. We are enamored with these temporary sensations. Instead, we should be focusing more on the work that we put in to create sustainable happiness—the means that lead to the end, which are in our control.

We thirst for validation, in order to feel appreciated—to be worthy, and to feel noticed. We calculate these things, but rarely, if ever, is there any personal assessment, in terms of what truly brings authentic happiness to each one of us individually. Why do we continue to assess our happiness based on these fleeting, unsustainable, external experiences? We are equipped with the internal power to ignite positivity in our lives. We can restructure the mind to find true success: happiness and love on our own terms.

The time is now—time to understand who you truly are and what makes you happy. Happiness can exist for all people and in all things. The time is now to identify the true nature and beauty of the person you see in the mirror. The time is now to enrich yourself with the communicational tools to strengthen bonds and the capacity to increase your love and acceptance for others.

Take control, choosing to be proactive each day in creating the way you feel and the person you want to become. Use authentic communication to spread happiness, allowing you to speak your dreams into reality.

What a blessing today is . . . Happiness is inside of us, waiting to be ignited. Today, we can begin asking the right questions, and start answering them truthfully. The happiness we once sought from the external is not what creates lasting happiness on the internal. Become unbreakable by developing sustainable happiness and cultivating your authenticity.

FINDING YOUR AUTHENTIC SELF

Years before proposing, I called my mom to ask her how she felt about my girlfriend, Agathe. As my relationship was becoming more serious, I sought my mom's insight and opinion and hoped that they could form a close bond. Mom answered without any hesitation; she highlighted some of Agathe's unique qualities and voiced some concerns she had about our relationship. You see, my wife is French, and our marriage meant that my career and family would be spread throughout three different countries—not to mention things like language barriers and cultural differences. None of these concerns were new to me; in fact, I'd already heard similar thoughts from friends and other family members. Days later, I was simply unsatisfied. I felt that her response was too generic. It reminded me of the hundreds of basketball pregame interviews I have done over the years, fielding questions about the other teams or players I was about to face and only giving a surface-level, public-friendly response. I called my mom again and challenged her to answer the question one more time. This time, I asked her to take some time to think deeply about Agathe and our relationship in order to respond authentically. Mom took days to respond, and what she realized in that time was that her initial thoughts on the matter had become routine and repetitive. She was giving the same response to me that she had given to her friends dozens of times before. When I asked her to answer the same question again, I challenged her to look into the character and authenticity of the woman I was dating, not just her surface-level attributes. I was also provoking my mom's authentic voice to be her only voice, eliminating external distractions.

When Mom took a bit more time, she was surprised by what she found. "I really love her," she told me. The surprise for her was not discovering that she loved Agathe; her surprise was finding that her authentic voice had been hiding behind generic ideas and surface-level feelings she had been programmed to feel. To truly evaluate feelings and understand who we are, we must dig deeper.

Why do we cover our true thoughts, our true emotions, and our true selves? What is stopping us from letting our most authentic selves shine through?

In his book, *Invisible Influence*, Jonah Berger writes, "Even when the answer is clear, people still imitate others." Berger's research focuses on the power of public influence and how it impacts the way we think and respond to the world around us. Jonah focuses on a study performed by Solomon Asch in 1951. Asch asked the subjects to decide which line, A, B, or C, matched the line on the left image. Why don't you take the time to choose for yourself.

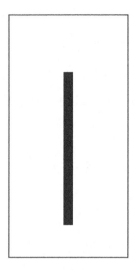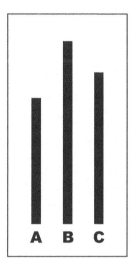

Participants in the study were asked to answer individually, and then asked the same question within a group setting. Some, or all, of the group members were planted as part of the experiment, actors positioned there to try to persuade thought and influence the test subjects.

"In sum, the situation was ripe with uncertainty. And when people feel uncertain, relying on others makes sense," says Berger.

What Berger found was that many individuals changed their original opinion when put into a group setting. They would ignore their instinct, simply to fit in with the group. Individually they would pick the letter C, but when put in a group, all answering with "B", many would change their answer to B, denying their authentic original answer. External influences have the ability to change our minds, altering our perception and beliefs. We consciously or unconsciously filter our lives, depending on who is in the room, as well as the social climate. Social pressures, and our desire to "fit in," cloud our mind, limiting our ability to give authentic responses and share our personal truth.

When I was in high school, I remember picking up a roll of film I had dropped off a week prior. I was filled with anticipation to see how the photos came out and to relive the experiences that were captured. I learned more about photography through my cousin, Shaw, who showed me how he developed all types of photos, including black-and-whites in a dark room, but things have changed since then.

Now, as soon as a photo is taken, we desire to see it in real time. We hone in on anything we don't like, deleting the unwanted images. We are now programmed to show the world a curated view of who we are. We use a preconceived standard to identify personal flaws that we don't want the world to see. Over time, we prefer not to see them either.

For the photos that do make the cut, don't worry, we can filter and photoshop out the small things we don't like. We begin with capturing a fun moment, and then programmatically filter the photo through a gauntlet of insecurity and external pressure clouding our mind. We increase the focus on ourselves, leaving out the beauty of a photo captured candidly. Finally, we post our doctored images, wanting the world to see who we are. But is that really us?

How authentic is your smile after the first photo? How about after you take the same photo five times to make sure you look okay? Ask yourself: How authentic is the "self" we are showing the world in this "selfie mode?"

We then think about what photos we want to share with the world. We take into account the audience and their potential feedback before we upload our images. We wonder; Will the audience loose interest if we don't promote a certain image, a certain way of life? We want to feel confident in what people will perceive instead of confident in who we are to begin with. Ask yourself the right question. Would you rather lose followers and friends, or lose yourself in the process?

You can only be appreciated for who you are, if <u>YOU</u> are the one on display. Is the person you see in the mirror a filtered, socially influenced version of you, or the real thing?

Who are you trying to please? Who benefits by showing this inauthentic version of yourself?

When there are multiple versions of yourself, you can become anxious and lost in translation; Who people think you are, who you claim to be, who you show on social media, who you try to be, and who you truly are. Create calmness within your mind and soul as you narrow down your worlds to become one true authentic reality.

Negative internal and external influences are the problem, not you. Who's to say that we aren't perfect just as we are, without filters or edits? Social influences appear in many different shapes and sizes, creating positive or negative energy in our mind. We must understand the magnitude of these voices and start evaluating their presence in our daily life. We need to filter out social influence on our happiness, before we think of filtering out our authenticity.

What voices are influencing your life?

Thinking back to my mom's initial response, when I asked her about Agathe, we can see how it reflected a filtered version of Agathe. When she removed the external pressure, my mom was able to discover and communicate who Agathe really was to her, using a new authentic lens.

We require a healthy balance in the way we filter the information that influences how we experience life. We must limit the power we give to people, places, and things, removing anything holding us back or creating doubt, anxiety, and fear in our life.

If you could define yourself using only one sentence, what would you say? If you could capture your true identity with only one photo, how would you look? Would your definition include your accomplishments and accolades? Would your photo capture who you are in your entirety? Have you been simplifying or showing just one facet of your multiple dimensions?

The ego is just one of the dimensions of your personality which you must understand, in order to know what it is you value, as well as who you are. The ego pushes us to excel in school. To date the prom queen. To get the highest-level job. To fight for the promotion, then the next promotion, then the next. We want to be proud of our effort and hope for validation and pride from our family and community. Our results must justify the means. Right?

When we keep our ego in check, we then wonder: Is happiness only found at the end of the road to success? Are we sacrificing who we are to get to where we want to be?

Thinking back on the last eleven years of my life, it's easy for me to question my own decisions, as I consistently choose to live far away from family and friends in my pursuit of happiness as a basketball player.

I have given up so much to be where I am today, so how am I any different?

The difference is, I've discovered that my success—my happiness— is found within my journey. With each choice and each moment, I choose to add pieces to who I am, instead of having them stripped away. While I may give up many moments, I will never give up who I am: **I am in the pursuit of success through happiness, not happiness through success.**

There has never been a more relevant time to reanalyze ego than 2021. The coronavirus required us to socially distance and exposed us for who we really are. Our titles and accolades that previously defined us have been redesigned. Our daily identity and societal roles have largely been put on hold or have been dramatically adjusted. We must reevaluate the person we see in the mirror, and get adjusted to our new role. As the world continues to redefine normalcy, we must focus on who we want to become in the wake of such a restructuring. We have the opportunity to remember what was important to us before the pandemic and reshape what will be important to us moving forward.

In this way, you can begin to identify who you are and who you want to be, and then create a life that is authentically you. Before you work toward it, you must first be able to envision it.

I was raised in a family that supported big dreams and encouraged my growth through imagination. Creativity was ingrained in who I was, and I spent countless hours on the basketball court imagining myself as a professional basketball player. I knew that I had to dream it first, in order for it to become reality. The next step for me was accepting that I could not yet be a professional basketball player at six years old, and I'd have to grow up a bit first. By age thirteen, I had realized that there were no quick fixes or easy roads on the path toward my success. I worked diligently to build my desired future, being active each day in creating my dream.

My thoughts, actions, and attitude have willed my dream into reality—one day at a time. It's easy to see that I don't look like the stereotypical basketball player. The average professional basketball player in the NBA is six feet seven inches tall and has a wingspan of six feet ten inches. Standing at six feet one inch "with two pads in each shoe," I've come to understand that I'm where I am today not solely because of my physical capabilities. There are players out there with more talent and more potential, who chose not to focus as hard or lacked the imagination and will to turn their dream into a reality. Most things worth having are worth fighting for, and come through a process, not from a handout. I often hear stories about the amazing potential of young players, or the wasted potential in other players. I hear comments like, "If she worked harder, she could have it all," or "If he believed in himself more, he'd be so much further in his career."

I worked harder than those more "athletic" than me. I worked smarter than those with more "potential." I used humility in what I couldn't control to strengthen the things I could. My path was not determined by comparing myself to what others perceived as a realistic path for someone of my physical attributes.

I am currently living out my dream for the second time. I've been here before. The first time was through my creativity and imagination as a child—the hours I spent dreaming on my driveway court. Now, I am empowered, reaping the benefits of what I sowed. I am the product of my effort and imagination, and physically living out the dream of playing professional basketball today, for the second time.

I strived for more, knowing that my success would not come at the failure of others, but in the power of my own desire and hard work.

It's imperative to stop comparing yourself and your situation to that of other people. If you need to compare, then try comparing yourself to the two most important people in your journey: who you are, and who you want to become.

No two lives are the same, and it is our personal privilege to seek out our own path. Your happiness is not found or evaluated based on the success of someone else. Only you have the ability to define yourself, through your words, your energy, your thoughts, and your actions. The world is full of opportunity, when you realize there is no "keeping score"—there is only learning how to enjoy the game.

Your ability to succeed in whatever metaphorical court you find yourself on is not based on potential; it's built on an internal desire and passion to excel. Be prepared to capture your dream by having the authenticity to identify it, imagination to think it, and the drive to turn opportunity into action. Be ready for all your "moments," big and small.

When I think about the path that led me to where I am today, I see my experiences like a roll of film; I captured every possible moment while going after my dreams. The world was not far behind whispering doubt and fear into my ear, but I wasn't going to let myself be affected by the noise. I was true to my path, not allowing external voices to influence my dreams. The moments captured on my roll of film are candid, authentic, and I work to appreciate the beauty of my journey and the authenticity that guided my path. My road has always been my own.

Many moments have assisted in creating who you are today, but none of them individually have the power to define who you are. You are a beautiful blend of all the moments that have collectively led you here. This is your starting point to finding daily purpose, passion, and happiness in your life.

There was only one road that got you here, but there are infinite opportunities and possibilities ahead. Your story is being written every day, and you must be the one holding the pen and actively writing. Define who you are, as the main character in your life, along with your individual characteristics and foundational values. If you don't define yourself, then your character is at the mercy of external influences and interpretations.

Well, here we are . . . We are heading back onto our respective courts—redesigned by a new time. Whether you are hosting dinner parties for friends you haven't seen in months, or going back to school or work, ask yourself this: Am I content with returning to the way I used to do these things? Was I authentic in the person I used to be?

Are you reevaluating what is important and how you can find your success and happiness?

We have an opportunity to define the time we live in. We have the ability to show courage through adversity. When the dust settles, will you become the person you desire to be?

Everything has changed. Have you changed for the better?

COMMUNICATION

"Great communication begins with connection. What makes us different from one another is so much less important than what makes us alike. We all long for acceptance and significance. When we recognize those needs in ourselves, we can better understand them in others, and then when we can set aside our judgments and just hear."

—Oprah Winfrey—

Communicating well is far from an exact science. Our intentions can be misunderstood, words misheard, and our meaning can be convoluted by diverse interpretations. Communication wields immense power. We all have the ability to create our own reality through communication with others and also with ourselves. Each day, you are influencing the world around you through the conversations you take part in. The way you communicate can inspire positivity, create space for deep listening, and encourage a new authentic voice. You can speak your desired future into existence.

Happiness is aided through the improvement of these five key areas of communication:

1. **Positive Soul Communication:** What are you telling yourself to build confidence and your sense of self?

2. **Listening:** Hear what the world is saying.

3. **Positive Filtering:** Interpreting the world through positivity and optimism—your new lens.

4. **Speaking with purpose:** How to best inspire others and create positive habits for ourselves.

5. **Communication in relationships:** Rooted in love and acceptance.

By adopting these five principles of communication, we have the ability to organically restructure our mind. Words have a gravitational pull, bringing people closer to their positive or negative energy. We can influence our world through the words we use, the way we use them, and the positive filter in which we interpret the words of others. First, we must understand the power and purpose in our own communication.

So how do we improve?

We must develop new habits, rooted in positivity and love. Communication thrives through an acceptance, respect, and appreciation for all people. Only when we understand one another are we equipped with the capability to communicate in a loving and positive manner.

The journey to successful communication begins with understanding the power of who is in the mirror and how you can use soul communication to unlock the happiness found within.

1. Positive Soul Communication

My dad once told me, "The quality of your life is based on the questions you ask yourself." It illuminates how internal conversations breed creativity and curiosity for life. Curiosity is the foundation of creating positive soul communication, opening an environment where you can discover who you are today and who you want to become tomorrow.

Soul communication is the inner dialog happening within your mind. What you're thinking, what you're telling yourself, and the thoughts you have about the world you live in, including how you think you fit into that world. Soul communication is as constant as a ticking clock, and we must acknowledge its power over our daily happiness.

What do I value? What is success and happiness for me? Do I have the courage to go find it? What obstacles are in my way, and how can I overcome them?

It is through this journey of asking questions like these—each based in curiosity—that you begin to find yourself. When you truly live within the journey, accepting who you are, and aware of all possible outcomes for your future, you begin to find your happiness in life.

Positive soul communication constantly promotes knowing, accepting, and loving the person in the mirror. When we look in the mirror, our eyes see what our mind has filtered and interpreted over years of programming and being subject to external influences. All around the world, stories are being told, rumors passed, and information shared, feeding into, and altering, our reality. In the same way, our personal reality of how we see ourselves can become a distorted version of truth, socially altered and influenced over time.

When you look in the mirror, what do you see?

There are layers of social influence: who you want to see, combined with your real reflection, personal ideology, and true self—your bare soul. Positive soul communication is about revealing that deepest, truest layer of yourself and connecting through conversations that promote happiness, confidence, and self-esteem.

Out of high school, I got a scholarship to attend Tulane University in New Orleans, Louisiana. The second day of my sophomore year, Hurricane Katrina devastated New Orleans, and altered my journey in life. Soon after, my basketball team was relocated to Texas A&M in College Station, Texas. I felt grateful to be safe but unsure of this unchosen and altered path that was forced upon me. I was determined to make the best of it, but within two months of being there, I tore ligaments in my right knee, ending my season. I watched my team from the sideline, unable to play the game I love, while attending classes at a school I had not chosen, living a life that didn't feel like my own. My cousin, Shaw, visited me during this time and acutely captured my visible internal struggle.

While I was recovering from this injury, I thought a lot about my future. After the semester in Texas, I would return to a rebuilding New Orleans with a torn knee. Near the end of the semester, I was told that the sports programs had little resources for my recovery. My heart was in Louisiana, but I had to make the decision to transfer, in order to get the support I needed to continue playing. I signed a new

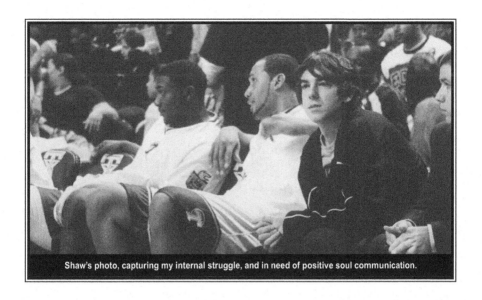
Shaw's photo, capturing my internal struggle, and in need of positive soul communication.

letter of intent to play, and attend, Washington State University. My arrival at WSU was less than impressive. I arrived on campus a few days after Christmas, to no welcoming committee, a snow-covered ground, and my recovering leg. Besides my assistant coach, I didn't know a single soul on campus. Despite all this, I was optimistic that my recovery would continue going well, and soon I could at least get back on the court. Well, I was wrong. Within just a couple of months of being at WSU, I was told that I needed a second surgery to repair the very same knee I was working so hard to recover. "Angry" would be a polite way to express how I was feeling upon hearing that news. Turns out that I was working too hard to recover from the first surgery, and my knee was not ready to handle the impact. I had spent months rehabbing, moved across the country to a new school, and now I faced starting another recovery all over again. My doctor spoke candidly with me and said that he didn't know if I would be able to continue to play again in a couple of months or even a couple of years. I feared the worst. My eyes welled up in sadness, as I imagined the pain I would experience before overcoming my situation. This could be a career ending injury. I felt low, both socially and athletically—stricken with the same face seen in Shaw's photo, every day. I needed to do some serious soul-searching to evaluate my situation, as well as my emotions.

My soul communication started with a simple message and a positive vision: Even when I am at my worst, I have the choice to envision my best.

The road wasn't easy, and I faced a new six-month recovery before being back on the court with my team. I was lonely and in pain, yet committed to speaking to myself, and about my situation, with strength and positivity.

Seemingly harmless questions like "How's the knee?" or "When will you be back playing?" tested my focus on staying positive.

I remained steadfast in my responses, highlighting my excitement for the future instead of my daily struggles or setbacks from the past. Positive soul communication changed the way I worked out, the way I spoke to others, the way I ate, the way I carried myself, and ultimately altered the way I interpreted happiness in my life. I spoke to myself about what it would feel like to be playing in a packed arena, or how I would feel being a part of the NCAA tournament at the end of the season. I spoke to myself about our team's future success, and encouraged my rehab process by thinking about how good my leg was feeling now, as opposed to thinking back on how bad it used to feel. I was consumed with speaking my positive future into reality, even if my future was uncharted and unknown.

Positive soul communication doesn't just impact you; it influences those around you, pushing the limits on what can be accomplished as a collective.

When I first arrived at WSU, my teammate, Daven Harmeling, and I spent a lot of time together; he was also rehabbing and sidelined with injury. During all of the home games that season, I sat with Daven, and we would often chat about the future. At one point, I looked around the stadium and turned to him and said, "Next year, everything is going to change—trust me. This place is gonna be full." For those who are unfamiliar with Cougar basketball history, the team was not so strong at that time in 2006. We were ranked low in the standings and didn't attract crowds, as we had a great team and individuals, but competed in an extremely challenging league that year.

Daven gave me a skeptical smile. He knew how difficult it would be to become a top team—not to mention, this was all being talked about by two players sidelined with painful injuries. When Daven and I returned to action, our coach, Tony Bennett, began the following season with a message: "TAY," which stood for "Turn Around Year." He, too, envisioned a new level of success. With this slogan ringing in our minds, Daven and I were infectious with our communication and confidence toward a winning path. We challenged each other each step of the way—in the weight room, in practice, and even with our studies—trying to encourage each other's performance in all aspects of life. This was a purely healthy form of competition, pushing each other to find the success that we envisioned when we first met. We focused on the power of each individual day, giving value to the journey, speaking positively of tomorrow's desired reality.

Three years later, we graduated from WSU after making the post-season three years in a row and our team being ranked as high as number four in the nation, at one point. I'll never forget the feeling of driving to the arena for our home games during my last season at WSU and seeing long lines of fans waiting hours before the game for the doors to be opened, remembering my first conversations with Daven. While there were many people who contributed to our success, I know one thing about our journey is certain:

We dreamed it, we worked for it, we achieved it—with positive soul communication.

Soul communication helps us stay mindful in the way that we act and react; we are slower to anger, slower to confrontation, and happier in daily interactions. When you see yourself, and your potential, in a positive light, the weight of the world is lifted from your shoulders. Imagining success doesn't require talent or take up added time and effort; it's simply a lens in which you control how you see the world through a happier projected version of yourself. Being able to hear your positive messages over any other noise changes the way you see yourself and also how you see the world.

To speak to yourself in the most productive and loving way is to always replace blame with love. **Blame deals with mistakes or troubles from the past, while love deals with forgiveness and acceptance, hopeful for a brighter future.**

Soul communication is the foundation of your happiest self, making it possible to take on a world of uncertainty, replacing anxiety with confidence.

When I am better at listening to myself, I create a positive environment, in order to be a better listener to others.

2. Listening

When Agathe and I first met, we did not speak each other's native languages fluently. She was learning English, and I spoke a few words of French. We spent a lot of our time intensely listening to each other, trying to get a true sense of who the other person was.

When I think about what made those early days in our relationship so special, I think of the curiosity we both felt for one another, which transformed deep listening into understanding. I wanted to know what she thought and felt, and, because of our language barrier, I couldn't possibly fill in the blanks or complete her sentences with my own opinions or assumptions. It was pure listening, as I literally had to hang on to every word, patiently. I learned to interpret her verbal communication, along with her body language, which aided my comprehension by picking up all her nonverbal cues. Most interestingly was that I couldn't listen to stories from others, or gather my own information by simply being in the room. I had to actively seek out anything I wanted to know.

Think about the idea of not having context to what people are saying—no preconceived notions of how you feel about something before you receive all the information; having to listen thoroughly enough before making your own conclusions; to actually listen to someone.

Too often, we don't fully listen, leading to an incomplete understanding of a topic, based on the preprogramming we have had our entire lives. It's time to truly learn before making assumptions or coming to conclusions. Realize that sometimes we need to listen before we speak.

Listening is not a passive experience, but rather an active role within the communication taking place. Being an active listener is not about preparing a response or thinking of ways to solve a problem. It's not an impatient ear gearing up to give unsolicited advice, which generally leads to misunderstanding intention. To be a true listener, we must be focused intently on hearing the information that is being shared with us, not waiting for our chance to hear our own voice in the conversation—to understand the person behind the message, the intent, and the message itself.

To be a good listener, you must be selfless and curious, knowing that, whatever differences or uncertainty you have with someone else, there is always room to gain knowledge and appreciation for other people. We have opportunities every day to learn *about* one another and to learn *from* one another. To be happy for one another, and to encourage healthy communication with one another. To use what we learn, and incorporate it into who we are, sharing purposeful messages to the world.

Listening doesn't require agreement—only acceptance, respect, and care for others. Listening is based in the realization that each and every one of us matter and deserve to be heard for who we are. Listening also provides a great opportunity to look inward, as your mind incorporates new insights and perspectives about your internal feelings and thoughts. My faith is strengthened by listening to people who share the same beliefs as much as when I listen to those with different beliefs. There is knowledge and truth in both sides of a story, not in the absence of one or the other.

We sometimes have a tendency to feel that we are already well-enough informed, and we can become agitated if we feel like someone is trying to teach us something or impose their beliefs on us. In this way, our own insecurities can alter our ability to listen deeply. We filter out what we consider to be unimportant and only hear the information that we feel is pertinent to us or comfortable to our preprogrammed beliefs.

Our minds are constantly overstimulated, making it hard to listen without making our own connections to the story or trying to insert our own experiences, thinking that we can relate to everyone all the time. We often drift into other thoughts and unrelated ideas, waiting for our chance to interject, interrupt, and share our two cents. It's not malicious, but when we are trying to relate to the speaker by sharing commonalities or connections with them, we sometimes aren't truly listening.

Are you listening to reply, or listening to understand?

I have to remind myself that, when people talk, it's not always about me. When my mind drifts, or I insert myself into someone's story, I play the wrong role in the communication, forgetting to realize that I'm not the focus. I must quiet my internal communication, in order to digest what is being said. I have to actively focus on not finishing other people's sentences. I must stop starting my sentence before the other person has finished theirs. This is how I show respect and curiosity to the speaker—how I value similarities and differences in all people, and how I learn alternative truths.

Think of the last time someone told you about an accomplishment of theirs. When you received the information, what emotions did you feel? Proud, envious, ecstatic, ashamed? Did you even hear the full story before your mind started to drift, comparing their story with one of your own? It's incredible to think that hearing good news about other people is not always good news to us. It can sometimes even put us in a bad mood. Imagine that . . . something is wrong here.

Remember, it's not all about you:

By listening without your own self-interference, you will be able to ask better questions and create space for deeper connection. This is where that curiosity you've been exercising while listening comes to fruition. You can cultivate an even deeper understanding by asking questions based on what you hear, instead of what you think you know. Ask about a culture you don't fully understand, growing in your complex knowledge of the world. Ask about the goals and dreams of other people, later being able to encourage them through support. Ask about their failures, and how they overcame them, helping you gain perspective and courage to overcome yours. Ask about what has shifted for them in the last year and what they hope to achieve in the one to come. Success is all around us, and we can use these moments of listening and asking questions to learn about ourselves along the way.

Another important skill of a listener is to be alert for self-destructive words. These words are born out of self-doubt and insecurity. It is important to be empathetic and sympathetic when we listen, but we also have a responsibility to acknowledge the role we play when we hear self-destructive communication. As a listener, you are the first line of defense for identifying self-sabotaging language, and should encourage reprogramming negativity into positivity. There is incredible power in the energy shared between listener and communicator. Listeners contribute energy through their curiosity and selflessness. Listeners offer reassurance through positive words, knowing that not everyone is practicing positive soul communication, and the communicator may be in need of external positivity.

Be a thought provider and thought provoker:

While actively listening, remember, there is a person behind the words. Stop nitpicking each example or opinion and, instead, get curious about the deeper messages that are being shared. Fight the urge to interject or shut down the conversations when you feel like you don't understand.

I remember telling a friend about a new diet I was trying. Halfway through my explanation of what I was eating, I realized that he wasn't even listening. I asked him where his mind was, and his response was self-demoting. He was filled with internal noise about his own body and his eating habits. He felt ashamed of his body and discouraged by his work ethic to take care of himself better. This type of response is what I like to refer to as "competitive listening."

When we shift the focus of listening to ourselves, we get lost in our own issues and assessing our own happiness through comparison and competition. Our minds wonder, "If other people are so happy and accomplished, then why am I not the same? Is something wrong with me and the decisions I make, the things I do?"

Cut it out. Being a true listener allows happiness to live and breathe within your conversation and shows the speaker that they are worthy of your time.

As a listener, you have the ability to create space for the speaker and their message—showing your curiosity to know more, taking authentic interest in other people. The best way to gain knowledge and understand the people around you is by stimulating new thoughts and encouraging them to open up about the things they know and the way they feel. Questions have answers, or may lead to entirely new and inspirational ideas. We are all filled with stories, knowledge, and ideas that will help us evolve into a more connected world. We just need to listen.

Listening is about affirmation. To affirm other people in who they are, and the importance of their message. Break down the barrier between reality and perception by getting real information. Learn before you judge, and be ready to be surprised by what you may find out.

3. Positive Filtering

Agathe likes to tease me by saying, "Taylor lives in the clouds." She's completely right, and I have come to take this as one of the highest compliments she gives me because it's reassurance that I continue to see the world in my own positive way.

I take all the information I encounter—by word or by sight—and find the best way to include it in my life, in a way that encourages happiness through "positive filtering."

Positive filtering is the ability to receive and interpret all forms of communication and information in a positive and constructive way. It's about hearing words in a positive tone and receiving people with pure intentions, to remove ego and to remain humble. It's a graceful understanding of "giving the benefit of the doubt," while being rooted in optimism and love for all people. This type of filter seeks out positive takeaways, refocusing uncertainty, in order to inspire love, not fear.

I know, I know . . . Wouldn't it be nice to always see the best in the world and the best in people? Pretty naïve, right?

If you think that this is impossible to implement as a daily choice, let's first dissect the truly irrational alternative.

The alternative to positive filtering is what I like to call, "guess-filtering." Yup, that's what you're doing each and every day. Guess-filtering is audaciously (and most likely inaccurately) assuming intent and guessing the meaning behind everyone and in everything you hear. If you're not positively filtering 100% of the time, then you are guess-filtering.

Guess-filtering is like trying to decipher an uncrackable code, leading to misunderstanding, frustration, and pain within conversations and interactions. It's why we struggle so much to remain consistent with our love and communication with one another.

Why do we allow so much of our happiness to be determined by a math problem that we can't solve?

I've experienced the negative consequences of guess-filtering first hand. I had an experience recently when I was texting with a friend and we had a misunderstanding. My friend was confused about what I had written, and instead of asking me directly, he found himself trying to determine the "tone of my text message." Wait, what? Are we more comfortable passively guessing someone's meaning than taking an active role in how we interpret the meaning? We get frustrated with one another, fight with one another, and even end relationships with one another over guess-filtering. How many of our daily conversations are being misconstrued, as we guess our way through almost all forms of communication.

I'm not saying that the tone of a message doesn't matter. I'm also not suggesting that everything we hear or read is meant with positive intent. But, when I choose to positively filter all messages, I limit communication breakdown by encouraging compassion in my relationships, while limiting my own internal struggle to solve communicational complexities. I create happiness through my positivity.

By positively filtering, I choose a world in which I control the effect that information and external influence has on me and the way I feel. I reveal my authenticity by finding critical feedback within criticism and silver linings within darkness. I counter negativity by focusing on the person, not the message. I choose to love the person instead of hating the message. Positive filtering is possible through the understanding that there are human beings behind words.

The summer of 2020 was a difficult time for me to be away from my home in America. From France, I watched footage of the powerful rallies promoting equality for all Americans. The news coverage was extensive, and I listened to countless hours of people misinterpreting messages, trying to dissect the meaning of others' words. The focus shifted from equality and the main message, to the difference in words used by each individual and the critics debating who is more correct or incorrect. We are all looking for the right words to use in the right moment. But our words, and the meaning that we give them, are not necessarily going to match someone else's interpretation and understanding. Words fall on diverse ears, as individuals carry different backgrounds, different understandings, and a different interpretation of the world itself. This incredible diversity is beautiful, but can lead to misunderstanding if we don't tap into positive filtering.

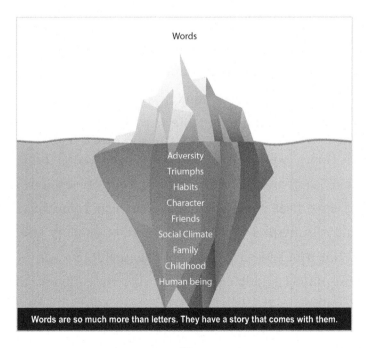

Words are so much more than letters. They have a story that comes with them.

Communication doesn't exist in a vacuum. Communication happens within layers and layers of context spanning from childhood experiences to the traffic we sat in just before meeting a friend. We have all had a bad day, felt pain, and experienced frustration. We have all said things we regret, used words that have hurt others. We all have a beating heart and find ourselves falling into heightened states of emotion, especially when it comes to the things we love and care about. We have mere moments to break down phrases, dissect emojis, and filter through our daily emotions before responding to the world around us. Our state of mind interprets the words we hear depending on how we are feeling at the moment. Seemingly straightforward words can be taken out of context or feel combative, when the people receiving them are not in a good mood. But, if I have to guess the intent and mood of every text or verbal conversation I have, I'm going to get a lot wrong, and drive myself mad in the process.

When you arm yourself with a positive filter, you proactively limit negativity and frustration from your daily life. No matter the source, no matter the words, images, or symbols, you control how the final message affects your state of mind moving forward. Ultimately, you control how all communication affects your happiness.

Taking a closer look at the 2020 Black Lives Matter rallies across the United States and around the world, I think about how amazing it would have been that, no matter what was being spoken, people would all interpret a positive message of equality and positive change. Not a mixed bag of negative connotations and misquotes from news outlets muddying up the true core intentions of the movement. Equality for all. Period.

As an athlete, Instagram has been a surprising platform for me to practice positive filtering with the messages I receive. Fans and critics alike frequently comment on my posts and send me direct messages after games. They're giving me a piece of their mind, and let's just say that some messages require a bit more positive filtering than others. I write back to critics, no matter the message, guided by positive filtering, with something like, "Thanks, I always appreciate feedback—hope you're having a good day." It's productive for me to redirect their criticism, knowing I create my own reality and can control how I allow it to affect how I feel. I am thankful to hear the opinions of others because I'm thankful that I am entitled to my own opinion, as well. I'm thankful for critics because I'm thankful for the career I am blessed with—one that has gained me critics in the first place. I'm thankful for my perspective, knowing the intent of my heart and that my hard work got me to where I am. It's important for me not to pick and choose the positive and negative things about what I do, but rather positively filter my world in its entirety.

After messages of positivity, it's amazing to see the responses I get in return. My positive words highlight the negativity in theirs, and also brings a context to the situation. My words serve as a reminder that there is a real person behind my words and actions, a human being on the other side of a username or profile. I give my heart to the game of basketball—the same heart I also like to show critics in times of their frustration. The truth is that, after a loss or bad performance, I could be equally frustrated, but I focus my energy on the future and on becoming better each day. I choose my reality.

Your positive filter is a key to communicating effectively and creating happiness. My career has been filled with countless potential misunderstandings. Between living in over ten different countries, traveling constantly for away games, and being surrounded by languages I don't speak, it's easy for me to be misunderstood. Being misunderstood is frustrating, whether it's about the way I feel, the person I am, or simply being misunderstood when I am trying to express myself. Every moment of every day has the opportunity for miscommunication or misunderstanding. I remind myself to focus only on what I *can* control.

My message is who I am, but if those around me are guess-filtering, I will naturally be misunderstood. If we guess-filter over and over, we lose our identity and create false identities in others around us.

If you find it challenging to interpret positivity within your daily communication, you may need to look at the types of conversations you have, and the people with whom you surround yourself. This is an indicator of the effect people have on you and the importance of surrounding yourself with more positive filtering speakers, thinkers, and communicators. Positive filtering creates an environment built on love and appreciation for one another. It impacts everyone around you—your coworkers, the teams you are a part of, your group of friends, and any place where you hold influence.

So, how does positive filtering play out in my daily life?

First, I go into each conversation with a fresh mind. Every conversation is one of a kind, and the only one that is happening now. **If I bring yesterday's mind into the reality of today, then I am losing out on the surprise and potential of each and every thing I encounter.** When my mind is fresh, then I am ready to listen and interpret new information, filter it, and make it my own. I actively surround myself with people and places that promote positivity, making it easier to filter out the negative, while compounding positivity throughout the day. I alter the songs on my playlist, the people I follow on social media, and the hobbies I spend my time on. My active involvement to create positivity is like adding wood to a fire: the more investment and trust I have in the flames growing higher, the happier I become, as my body is warmed by what it needs to find inspiration and optimism.

So, choose:

Keep guessing, misunderstanding, and confounding, claiming to know truth in its entirety and having access to all the information throughout history, in order to understand the intent and substance of every piece of information that we receive for the rest of our lives . . .

(or)

Add positive filtering and transform your life, bringing you more and more happiness every day.

You are now armed with a filter that can change your mind and increase your happiness. It's time to use your words to change the world around you and inspire happiness in others.

4. Speak with purpose:

"It took me quite a long time to develop a voice, and now that I have it, I am not going to be silent."

—Madeleine Albright—

Words are the building blocks that construct our world, giving shape, color, and contour to what we experience. Speaking with purpose is about aligning your words to your values and intentions. Purposeful communication inspires, encourages, and strengthens conviction and authenticity. We have the power to live out the change we desire, by giving our words purpose.

A purposeful voice is filled with inspiration instead of instruction. **Motivation instead of manipulation.** Celebration instead of criticism. Dreams and optimism instead of fear.

More than ever before, we need to understand the power our voices hold and our capability to effect change with our words. In the same way COVID-19 spread rapidly throughout the world, our voice has the power to ignite a flame that can spread like wildfire. Through social media, each of us now has access to the world's loudest and most powerful microphone. With great power comes great responsibility. Your broadcast has the potential to spread love, fuel inspiration, and cultivate optimism, but it's also powerful enough to instill fear, hate, and judgement in the world. Speaking with purpose is actively fighting fear and eliminating blame, while echoing positivity, even in the face of injustice. Your audience is listening . . . Are you ready to communicate a purposeful message that you can be proud of?

Tolerance and understanding:

It took traveling the world and engaging with diverse people and cultures for me to understand the difference between information and fact. Webster's Dictionary defines a fact as: "Reality; actuality;

truth." My experience taught me that a student in Greece learns different facts than a student in Germany. Something that is known and something that is perceived are two very different things.

Hope for a better understanding through communication rests in "factual context" and the purpose of our words. We navigate through shallow waters of similarities and deep waters of fundamental differences. We must have tolerance for the voice and opinions of others, using our own opinions to help build understanding rather than judgement.

Judgment leads to divisive words. Tolerance redirects frustration that stems from a difference in opinions; we experience and share tolerance through the acceptance of others, learning and evolving in each interaction.

Highlighted happiness:

A purposeful foundation to your day starts with giving voice to the blessings you are experiencing in your life. I remember studying for tests—normally the night before the exam—when I was in school; I spent the night highlighting important information in order to remember what was needed to pass the test. Once the test was finished, I would simply move on with my day and on to the next test. The highlighted material would become the lasting imprint in my mind as I moved on to other topics in other classes. In a similar way to how we store these memories so they can be recalled, we can also create space for our daily happiness to be at the forefront of our mind. So, highlight your happiness by starting each day with your blessings, infusing positivity in your words and in your mind.

Create a habit of highlighting your blessings to yourself, and consider sharing them publicly to your loved ones or on your social network. This habit of sharing gratitude creates an indestructible foundation of what's important in your life.

Highlighting happiness is not about ignoring the negativity in your life, but rather about creating a healthy balance and perspective to carry you through your day.

A healthy balance, led by gratitude for your blessings, gives strength in times of adversity, providing you with a familiar vocabulary of uplifting encouragement.

Speak positivity into existence:

Listen to the way you speak—the tone you use and the words you choose—and acknowledge the effect it has on others, including yourself. Have you noticed your own personal habits toward the way you mix words, phrases, and vocal tones? Are you more often voicing positivity or negativity?

Think about all the amazing stories you have shared throughout your life. Stories told over time have the ability to take on alternative narratives, depending on the storyteller. While facts may be facts, our memories have a way of altering the past, as time goes on. Our memories are tricky and have a tendency to turn little alterations or embellishments into fact. In most cases, this is harmless, but you can imagine the alternative, and see why speaking with purpose and positivity can be life-changing.

We don't have the ability to change the past, but, over time, our perception of the past, told through a positive narrative, can create a happier and more empowering story.

Similar to highlighting your happiness, if you constantly tell stories that speak of the good moments and the positives that you took from them, your memories of the past will alter in a positive way. Your mind redirects the adversity you faced, showing strength in your fight and empowerment through the lessons you learned, not the adversity itself. You can change the narrative by infusing positivity into your story, creating a more fulfilling yesterday, today, and tomorrow.

Don't give (bad) advice:

"Advice is a form of nostalgia. Dispensing it is a way of fishing the past from the disposal, wiping it off, painting over the ugly parts, and recycling it for more than it's worth."

—Mary Schmich—

"The difference between the right word and the almost right word is the difference between lightning and a lightning bug."

—Mark Twain—

Never underestimate the power of the advice you give to other people. Don't take for granted the responsibility of listening and needing to provide others with words of advice. Too often, we provide shallow advice or half-thought-out responses, taking the path of least resistance, devaluing communication. We like to tell people what they want to hear, or fear the consequence of speaking truth. When you don't have a proper response, or can't find the positivity in your words, have the humility to say, "I hear what you're going through, but I'm not sure how to respond." We can show how much we love and care for one another by the quality of time and effort we give them. Take the time to formulate your advice only after listening deeply, removing your own baggage, and creating space for positivity and truth. Speak purpose into the lives of others and inspire positivity for their future.

Complaining:

One of my favorite childhood activities was the card game, Go Fish. I've found that adults like to play the same game, only now, we substitute the normal playing cards with daily complaints from our everyday lives.

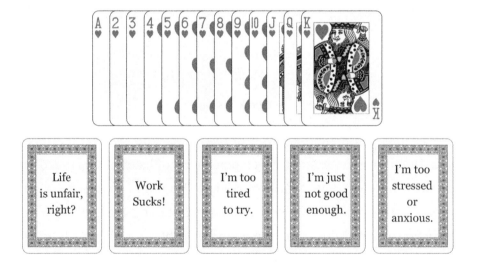

We carry around our complaints each day, searching for others to play the game, sharing our complaints or aiding in making our complaints stronger. We project our complaints on other people, like asking for a card, seeking someone, anyone, to commiserate with us. If the other person is uninterested in our pity party, then we "Go Fish" and pull out a new complaint in hopes that they may share in that pain. If all else fails, we move along and seek an empathetic ear elsewhere, and continue playing.

Complaining is one of the most destructive and digressive habits one can have, yet it has become commonplace. We feel obligated to share complaints with anyone who will listen, including ourselves. We find a twisted sense of pleasure in voicing our dissatisfaction.

We need to put a leash on complaining—only allowing complaints the minimum distance and space they require. Recognize the length of your complaints and the consistency in which you spew negativity on yourself and onto others. Recognize why, and when, it's occurring and commit to limiting the amount of time you let yourself stay in your frustrations. Often, one complaint leads to another, and we must find ways to stop the pattern before it builds.

Consider this: when you constantly complain about your boss, then your brain starts to interpret that you are unhappy with your job. If you're constantly feeling unhappy about your job, where you are spending a significant amount of time and effort, then your brain interprets that you are less content with your life in general. Following this rabbit hole, your words create a foundation of constant dissatisfaction. Limit your complaints, creating the necessary space to invite positivity in.

While in confinement during the Covid-19 pandemic, I remember thinking, "Man, I'm looking forward to getting back to my normal complaints."

Witnessing the global suffering that the virus caused provided perspective, as I realized that my small complaints are a luxury. If you find yourself stuck on a small complaint, redirect your energy to remembering the perspective gained from being aware of the bigger picture.

Yeah, but . . .

"Yeah, but . . . life isn't always so good."

"Yeah, but . . . I'm pretty busy and don't have time to worry about my happiness."

"Yeah, but . . . I'm not that good at what I do, and I don't like my job."

"Yeah, but . . . what if I fail?"

We often cut happiness off before we give it room to grow. Our mind is programmed to limit our excitement and, instead, squash our reality with words of practicality. Fill your language arsenal with confidence, letting your words fight off your complaints and fears of the unknown. Recognize your overuse of "yeah, but . . ." and how that phrase constricts your mind's ability to explore with optimism.

"Yeah, but . . ." is the foundation of sitting in complacency, not reaching for more. We must eliminate this habit and find new ways to respond, in order to divert away from the negativity of "yeah, but . . ." and create opportunity and excitement for whatever comes next.

Finding the "perfect" in imperfection:

The problem is, most people don't think they are complainers. They are simply not awake to the idea that it's a big part of the way they communicate. Complaints often come in the form of nitpicking the "now." We tend to compare whatever is happening now with a hypothetical idea of perfection.

Each summer, my wife and I review the contract offers that come my way for the upcoming season. Our decision process includes assessing pros and cons, and if I'm lucky enough to have two or more contracts, we compare and contrast the potential future situations. After playing overseas for so many years, I recall past personal experiences of the cities, players, coaches, and new information I have on each team I am considering.

In my mind, I create the "perfect" situation. I envision an incredible deal financially, in a perfect city, with perfect teammates and coaches. I want a perfect house waiting for my family, the perfect car to drive me there, incredible neighbors, and a fun community for my kids to play in. Then, with the "perfect" situation in mind, I stop and breathe.

I take a deeper look at my options. Maybe the city is not my top pick, or I am being offered less money than I made in previous years. Once I make a decision, I find myself making justifications for my decision that are rooted in my own insecurities. Throughout my career, I've felt more and more pressure to stay at the top of my game and play for the best teams or be open to critics wondering what has gone wrong. My concerns can quickly devolve into complaints about what could have been, if I allow them to perpetuate. Complaints don't stop after my decisions are made; they linger around each corner, waiting for me to experience any type of adversity so they can seep negativity into my thoughts and words.

What about all the amazing things that are included in my new contract? Another year playing the game I love? Seeing a new country and being part of a new culture? I fall into thinking that my new team is not as good as my last team. My new city is colder than the other city I could have chosen. My new team practices way too much, and my coach is crazy. My body hurts.

I'm tired of this shit. How can I stop this complaining since I know it is destructive and limiting my personal growth? I imagine my perfect situation, and then I digress with complaints if reality doesn't add up.

Self-doubt finds every crack it can, and attempts to creep in and question everything about the situation: "If I had just been given the right opportunity, things would be better. Maybe I should have made a different decision." My focus is diverted toward thinking about that damn grass on the other side of the fence.

Enough is enough. Give yourself a minute, fifteen minutes, whatever time you feel is truly necessary, and get it out, but don't let your negativity solidify into the foundation for how you experience your life. Acknowledge that negativity and frustration exist, but only in order to build strength from them. In this way the positive foundation of your communication is like a tree trunk, with complaints making up just a few weak branches, or better yet, falling leaves.

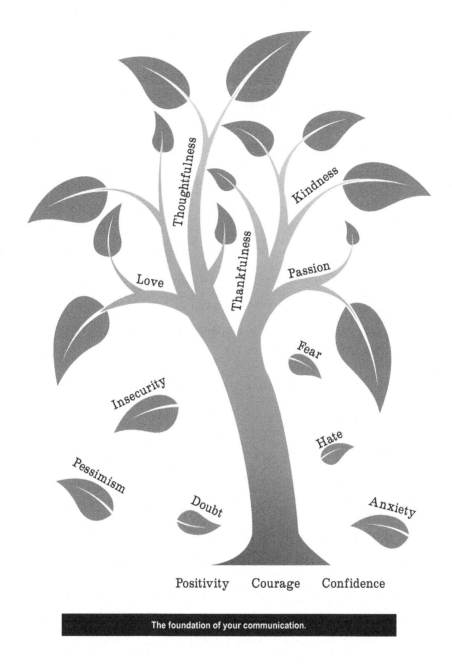

The foundation of your communication.

Let the leaves fall where they may, soon to be raked away, while you stay rooted in positivity, courage, and confidence.

Saying "sorry":

Some people don't have a problem with "sorry," while others fall into one of two dangerous categories:

1. Those who don't say "sorry," and probably should more often.

2. Those who say "sorry" too much, and probably should say it less.

For those who don't say sorry, this is another opportunity to put your ego aside. Words have the ability to pierce the skin and hurt others deeply. On the other hand, most issues can be resolved with words. Whether you're fixing a wrongdoing or remedying a damaged relationship, a genuine "sorry" can help you create space for relationships to deepen and flourish, while also developing the quality of your character.

Others use "sorry" a little too much. When you say you're sorry too often, you're showing the world that you believe you're letting someone down, or not living up to expectations they have. Never be sorry for who you are and what you believe in when your actions and words stem from kindness and love for another. Eliminate self damaging thoughts, telling you that you're not good enough, or smart enough, to have a powerful, unique voice. There should be no "sorry" for authentic contributions. Fear leads some to bite their tongue when they should feel empowered to speak their truth. If you bite your tongue enough times, you may end up biting it off completely.

Fuel your engine, not the fire:

Our words are like fuel—able to power the engine of inspiration or spark flames of negativity all around us. The most insidious type of negative communication is bullying.

My godfather, Todd Langerveld, shared a story with me when I was in college that transformed the way I think about bullying. He remembers being at a football game with some friends during his college days. His buddies were making fun of a girl who was sitting a couple rows ahead, and Todd joined in. They went back and forth, using disrespectful words that added fire to a flame that was gaining momentum. He turned toward another friend mid-laughter, looking for reassurance and potentially more fuel to add to the fire. Todd recalls his friend looking back at him with disappointment and empathy for the girl who they were making fun of. Feeling like a sunken ship, Todd vividly remembers the feeling of shame, vowing to never take part in bullying ever again, and stand up for those who he saw being bullied. I realized that bullying has so many forms, seeming so harmless and comfortable in the moment. Simple words turn into actions, often repeating themselves until they become habits.

Are you using your words to agree with the majority?

Be confident in your authentic voice, even when it sounds different from what you're surrounded by and used to hearing. Be steadfast in creating your own message. Never speak ill of another person, especially when they are not in the room. There are no positive outcomes achieved by knocking someone else down. When we speak with negativity about others, we build walls, exclude and separate ourselves from them. When we speak with positivity and purpose, we speak to enhance life, to bring love to our reality, and promote inclusivity. We are in dire need of inclusiveness, understanding, and connectivity. Be part of the solution, part of building a better future, and part of living out the change you want to see for the next generation.

Positivity and love, or fear and pessimism . . .
What is your message?

Just about every news outlet uses a fear-based approach. Fear strongly influences viewers, oftentimes causing a divide. Democrats and Republicans sometimes forget they are both Americans. Christians and Jews sometimes forget they are both faith-based. This is no political call to action or call to prayer, but a stress on the importance of communication.

Communication only needs one agenda—the promotion of love, kindness, compassion, unity, and happiness for an inspired today, hoping to inspire a better tomorrow.

The news has chosen its preferred style, using their influence to promote their concerns and ideas for the future. We, too, have our own platform, which we can use to promote the communicational changes we want to see—authentic information, promoting happiness and love as our main platform. A positive filter, using words of encouragement, inclusion, and finding new ideas that bring people together. Less "them" and "they," and more "us" and "we."

Words matter. Ask for the things you need and be clear about the things you want. Your words design your truth. They are your message. They are your authenticity. They create the future.

5. Communication and the necessity of relationships

"To effectively communicate, we must realize that we are all different in the way we perceive the world and use this understanding as a guide to our communication with others."

—Tony Robbins—

From intimate connections to new acquaintances, all relationships hold the power to inspire and create raw and influential energy. We rely on these relationships to make us feel our connection to one another, through similarities and differences.

2020 shook up the world, redefining the way we interact and communicate with one another. COVID-19 showed us the power (and the potential peril) of connectivity and how small the world has truly become. It has taught us that we do, in fact, all share vulnerability and rely upon one another, in order to remain safe and healthy, both physically and emotionally. Relationships must inspire each individual to be better and express care for one another, helping to collectively create a better tomorrow.

Are you passionate about developing and nourishing relationships in your life? What's getting in the way of you developing and maintaining deep bonds?

When we seek personal achievement or focus too narrowly on other pursuits, we neglect the very thing that brings happiness into our lives. Relationships are easily dismissed in our attempt to bring other passions to fruition.

Relationships may be complex and challenging, but they should never be defined as "hard." Life brings hardship. Connectivity, through relationships, makes life easier and ultimately happier. Try not to mistake the two.

So how do we develop deep, intimate, and mutually fulfilling relationships?

Start by turning away from technology and being more reliant upon face-to-face social interaction. Tap into your relationships to discover recommendations, advice, or encouragement in your life. TV, Google, Amazon, and Instagram are amazing; however, they can't be your best friend and certainly shouldn't be teaching you everything about life or overly influencing your happiness. The more time we spend on screens, the less time we have for one another, making true human connectivity obsolete.

Now more than ever, human connection is vital to our happiness.

We need to open our hearts toward one another and remember the importance of creating relationships and connections that are not just read or heard about but connections that are felt.

Have you ever been to Las Vegas and sat down at a blackjack table with friends? Blackjack players lose more when they only play for themselves and give into social influence, personal doubt, and fear. What most blackjack players don't know is that, when they all work together, the likelihood of winning increases for everyone. For most people, the answer to relational happiness is not found in Vegas, but through what we learn in the metaphor. Healthy communication in relationships does not focus on the happiness of individuals. Relational happiness is found in the journey toward the success and happiness of the entire group, or all involved.

The best way to understand relational happiness and implement it in your daily life is to visualize a one-way freeway—this is our "relational freeway." If we hope to create a healthy love for one another, our relational freeway must close off all off-ramps and throw out all shortcuts. A relationship that includes off-ramps and exit signs leads to selfishness and self-survival, opening the opportunity for abandonment or "checking out," which leads to insecurity for both parties. On the contrary, relationships with no off-ramps inspire a shared objective—one goal that promotes healthy communication based on desired mutual success.

"Exits" and "off ramps" represent the idea that the relationship can be broken at any moment, as any individual may decide to go off on their own, break up with a loved one, or stop being friends with someone else. Relational exits lead to destinations that may or may not include others, potentially leading to isolation, confusion, argumentation, and distrust within relationships. The fear of abandonment, or being alone, is enough to put pressure and stress on a relationship. Knowing we have the ability to walk away from people provides power to treat them in a negative or disrespectful way. This perceived power creates an imbalance within the relationship that plays out in the way you communicate and act toward other people. Off-ramps and exits are felt just as much as they are seen. When a relationship is dictated by the goals of individuals, one can take an exit or leave the relationship at any moment and forge their own path, unscathed by the separation damages. This is especially problematic and damaging when there is constant exiting and entering throughout the relationship.

When your relational freeway doesn't include exits and off-ramps, and all of the fear of isolation and insecurity that comes along with them, there is just one destination: being together. When my wife and I have an argument, or reach a tough moment, we are unwavering in the agreement that our road will always lead to "us" being together. This changes the very foundation and nature of problem-solving and conflict resolution, with the knowledge and comfort of knowing that "we" will always be "we," bringing added trust and security to our relationship. The power of "we" directly focuses on resolution, having no mind space for "right and wrong."

Successful relationships are mutually beneficial and promote the health and happiness of all included. Those in successful relationships seek a destination together, work together no matter the obstacles, and are secure in feeling they are not alone.

It's also important to note that not all relationships are worth holding onto. People change and evolve, sometimes requiring us to seek new relationships, in order to protect ourselves and our future growth. Your journey is your own, and you must choose wisely who you bring with you on your path. When you have the people around you who promote your well-being, then you will naturally create a shared path toward happiness.

I have seen this concept play out in sports teams, businesses, and other groups looking to develop stronger connections and healthier relationships rooted in happiness and self-confidence.

Imagine the difference you will feel sitting next to a coworker, knowing you will be working alongside them for the next thirty years.

Imagine if your success was also based on their success. Would you be more encouraging and more helpful when you interacted with them? Would you be more loving toward one another, using different words to help promote courage and positivity? We can find strength in knowing that all obstacles can, and will, be overcome in a way that promotes the whole rather than the individual, ultimately lifting both to a higher level than was possible individually.

I often think, "How do people know that Agathe and I are married?" If someone were to observe and listen to us in a group setting, would they notice a difference in the way we treat one another, compared to people who are just acquaintances? With my friends, how are we treating each other, and is it any different than an interaction with a stranger?

We have the ability to inspire and find the best in one another, when we take the time to realize the people who matter to us and treat them in a way that they understand their value. We can use this same strategy, even with strangers, as our love and care for the world becomes foundational to who we are.

Always highlight strengths, or be a compliment to perceived weakness:

Each unique characteristic of an individual makes them who they are. We all come into relationships with perceived weaknesses and strengths that we must be willing to accept and compliment in one another. Learning to highlight strengths includes the ability to speak highly of someone else, bringing them self-worth and security, as a cared-for human being. Positive words motivate and provide energy, empowering people to see the qualities in themselves that you cherish in them.

Soul communication taught us to pick out the best qualities in ourselves and promote happiness from the inside out. Externally, we learn about one another through listening and understanding what they bring to the table. Use this understanding to highlight strengths and encourage individual uniqueness. Your words help support and affirm others' positive soul communication.

Affirmation should be heard and felt both privately and publicly:

Public verbal affection has extremely meaningful and lasting effects. During American wedding ceremonies, there is often a time when the bride and groom exchange vows with one another. This display of love, through words, is shared in front of family and friends for a reason. The intimacy of sharing vows in public creates a shared experience and affirmation of love. Expressing our love for one another doesn't require an altar or even a formal celebration. You can affirm the qualities you cherish in others every single day, inspiring future happiness through the acknowledgement of your appreciation for them. These seemingly small efforts can have a big impact. If we desire improvement in our relationships, we must be able to recognize effort and show our appreciation.

Give voice to what can be done, instead of what's not being done:

Be cautious in telling others how they should do something or how you would do something. Instead, refocus your words toward suggestion and affirmation rather than criticism and judgement. Eliminate negative blanket statements like "he always" or "she never"—these types of judgments leave little room for healthy growth.

Blanket statements water down the unique value of each individual. It's easy to think, "Finally, he listened; I have been asking him to do that forever" or "She is always lazy." The truth is, when you put someone in a box of "always" and "never," then you are focused on what's missing, not encouraging what's already there. **Love does not grow by telling people who they are and who they are not. Love is found through encouraging them to be the best person they can be, while valuing who they already are.**

Blanket statements eliminate thankfulness. Instead, communicate specific intentions with one another, expressing your feelings toward the small things and why they are important to you. Relationships cannot rely on mind reading and guessing.

It helps to think like this: Start each day with a clean slate, then, if someone makes a mistake or irritates you in a small way, it's the first time they are doing it, not the 100th time. Each moment becomes the "exception," not the rule. Positive change comes through being able to accept small triggers each day and redirect them toward healthy communication instead of explosive frustrations.

Communicating with love and affirmation:

I feel extremely fortunate in having a mother and father who constantly spoke to my brother and I with love and affirmation while we were growing up. Even now, just about every phone call or conversation I have with my mom or dad ends with some form of, "Is there anything else I can do for you?"

As a husband, father, family member, and friend, I realize the importance of checking in and showing that you are there for your loved ones. These communicational patterns and thoughtful words create a foundation of confidence and self-esteem to those absorbing your love and affection.

For those who didn't experience this level of love and affirmation in their upbringing, we can't change the past, but we can change the future with how we communicate with one another. Every day, we get to choose our words, so let's choose love and affirmation. This style of communication is contagious and valuable in all types of relationships, as we learn about the people around us, picking up cues and finding ways in which we can add security and love into their lives.

"I love you" or "I care about you" is a great start to any conversation. Adding simple positive phrases like: "I'm never too busy for you," "Anything you need, I'm here for you"; "Talking to you always makes my day better" creates a healthy environment for your relationships to grow and deepen.

Take every opportunity to let the people you love know that you are proud of them, care for them, and appreciate them. Communicate love and affirmation, even with people you don't know or people that you sense may be in need of some form of love or comfort.

When you receive words of love and affirmation, don't take them for granted; receive them with thankfulness, knowing it's not commonplace for everyone to share those feelings—it is a blessing to hear.

Challenge one another:

Healthy relationships blossom when we are challenged by one another and open to positively accept each challenge. There is no way I could have gotten to where I am professionally without the pressure and encouragement to work harder in becoming better. My first professional coach told me that he wanted to find ways to push me outside of my comfort zone, even to the point of frustration, in order to get the best out of me and find out what I'm capable of.

Individually, we may resort to feeling comfortable, but collectively, we must be held accountable, to reach for higher levels, or to remain steadfast when we're on a good path. Remember, challenging others comes with the responsibility of challenging yourself. Hold yourself accountable for that which you hold others accountable.

Communicate intentions to get on the same page:

While living in Tel Aviv one season, Agathe and I hosted a Thanksgiving dinner for all of my teammates and their families. This was the first Thanksgiving that my wife fully prepared and hosted the entire meal herself. When the night was over, I was filled with thanks and praise, congratulating my wife for hosting such an amazing event.

She looked at me and said, "You thought it went well? It wasn't at all what I expected."

While we both had a great time, she felt let down by the night not living up to her expectations of what Thanksgiving dinner would be like. She envisioned sitting around a big table and hearing from each individual about what they were thankful for. Traditionally, this is the way my family did it, the way I talked about it, and the way she expected it to go. However, since I had been overseas playing basketball, I had come to accept that the traditions I grew up with wouldn't be the same, depending on the country we were in and the friends we celebrated with. Overseas, the Americans and some international players on my teams, usually would get together and share a fun night in a more casual way. Most of the places I played, I rented an apartment for the season with a small dining table, and rarely had a teammate with a large house and a table big enough to sit ten to twenty people.

Finally able to host, Agathe was really looking forward to having time to get to know each guest and looking forward to sharing in this tradition. Our main dining table wasn't big enough to seat everyone, so we were scattered all around the apartment, enjoying food and each other's company in groups of two or four. The team had practiced that day, and people showed up for dinner at different times, some coming straight from practice, and the others coming after rehab or picking up their families. All in all, it ended up being more of a party than a traditional Thanksgiving dinner.

This dinner helped my wife and I to grow, and gave us a chance to learn about how we create expectations, and cope when experiences don't match up to what we expected.

We must invest deeper in one another and take time to learn about the people we care about, in order to be their strongest support system in any circumstance. Or at the very least, you can laugh about it together, later.

Take a moment to understand your expectations and goals for the day. Learn about the dreams and aspirations of the people around you. As you grow in your understanding of other people, you can become more equipped to handle all types of surroundings and encounters.

Cut the blame:

"So, you don't want to go out tonight?" "You didn't text me back." "So, you didn't call the potential client?"

At first glance, these may seem like fair questions or statements, but speaking in negatives creates animosity, bringing negative energy to the situation and the relationship. Resentment forms through communication that's condescending and spiteful. If someone isn't calling, just call them, or let it be. If your coworker forgot something, it doesn't help to add on your frustration. Little negative sound bites like these create an energy that impacts the happiness within the relationship. The energy you feel is what motivates the next words you wish to speak. You can see how this type of negativity can quickly spiral out of control. Be clear in your intentions, purposeful in your words, and communicate with positivity to help build each relationship.

Stop comparing:

We compare friends, lovers, and strangers. We compare our loved ones to who they used to be, or who we thought they were.

"You used to be this or that," "You don't do this anymore."

Projecting these comparisons doesn't do any good for anyone and, instead, forces them to contemplate thoughts of not living up to expectations, creating anxiety and tension. Focus on what can be done, never what's missing, continuing to build positive relational habits.

Bottled identity:

Feelings are not meant to be bottled up inside you. We often hold back little frustrations, in order to keep the status quo, not wanting to shake up a relationship. Looking for positive alternatives to expressing our frustrations may take time, and we must not lose our identity or compromise our authenticity in the meantime. While you're busy saying things like "whatever," "I don't mind," and "I'm fine," you are choosing a repetitive habit of not communicating true feelings when opportunities present themselves. Bottling up your feelings takes away from your authentic expression, leading you further and further from your true self. Speak your truth and maintain your presence in all your relationships. When you speak with purpose that's layered with kindness, you shouldn't be afraid to open up and share your thoughts, as you're speaking to create an outcome of positivity for the whole.

Disagreements may be challenging and confrontational, but they are also an opportunity for understanding, learning, and appreciation. Enrich your relationships by learning a new perspective or idea from someone else. Communication—especially disagreements—are never about choosing a winner and a loser. The only way to win is if the "team" wins.

Sadly, most people would rather be "right" than happy. There is a constant desire to "one-up" other people to prove a point. When we face fight or flight, instinctively we defend ourselves, bullying or attacking others to gain the higher ground. What's your desired goal? Winning the argument or solving the issue? Have the fortitude to see past the issue, allowing your words and your focus to be on the relationship, not the momentary argument. See past the now, in order to build a better future. Remember, you're sharing the same road. Make sure you're all moving in the right direction.

Take ten:

What do you do when conversations get a little too intense?

You take ten.

When you truly cherish your relationships, then you can notice when someone is just not in the right headspace for the conversation or needs a minute before continuing the discussion—and that person who needs time might just be you. Take a moment and be strong enough to give a moment to someone else.

I remember how I felt during, and after, my first major disagreement with Agathe. At the time, the issue felt like life or death. Truthfully, as I'm writing this, I can't remember what we even fought about, but I remember how it was resolved. Some arguments end without finding common ground or some form of conflict resolution that satisfies both parties. Sometimes, arguments can be ended without the need for understanding or agreeing.

In this case, we created our own end to the argument, realizing that what was *mutually* beneficial was also *personally* beneficial. We decided to stop talking, got in our car, and drove to the beach. We ran as fast as we could and jumped in the ocean, cleansing ourselves from the argument and the negative atmosphere we had created with our words. The cold Pacific water gave us the awakening that was needed to clear our mind and create a fresh start. Sometimes, the best way to compromise and find a solution is to create one that is totally unrelated. Problems are eventually solved, tensions rise and fall, and we need to understand the power of our words, often saving them for the right time—after the waters settle.

Avoid communication blockers:

We can encourage positive communication and connection by avoiding blocking phrases like "you don't understand," "doesn't matter anyway," or "whatever." These communication blockers put a box around the conversation, effectively limiting it from going anywhere. We use blockers in times of frustration, exhaustion, or having a lack of desire to give energy to one another.

If someone doesn't understand you, search for the words that might explain your position, instead of shutting them out for not understanding. Communication is inclusive, welcoming, and educational. Try to listen, with the curiosity of being on a first date, while you speak as if you've been friends or married for years. When you remove these blockers in conversations, you allow words to bear fruit, inspiring new thoughts and leading to new discoveries together.

During the first couple years of our relationship, Agathe and I had to find interpretive ways to communicate with one another. I was patient while she learned English, and she patiently translated for me during our time spent in France, with her French-speaking family members. I used stories to explain English sayings and phrases, while she fielded question after question, pausing to interpret and make sure everyone felt heard. There were thousands of moments where we could have just ended our communication, opting to not put in the work to understand and be understood. For us to understand each other, and communicate with our families, we decided to give one another the effort and focus that was required. Today, we continue to choose to fight for one another each day, always keeping our line of communication open to one another, knowing that our connection is critical to our mutual happiness.

Find the moments in your busy day:

Living in Europe and Asia for so many years has taught me to be intentional with the way I communicate and the time I spend with others. I spend less overall time with the people I grew up with, only seeing them in the summer when my season is over or during short visits with friends a family. I must make every moment a priority and fill them with quality and thankfulness. I try to carry this over in my daily life, as well, adding intention and quality to the things I say and do. I have spent hours talking with people on the phone and spent quality time with visitors. I like to think that a week spent with someone who is visiting me carries the same impact on a relationship as seeing someone once a week for the entire year. When we see each other casually or routinely, we lack the purpose and intention, knowing that we'll see them again sooner or later. With my lifestyle, I have to be intentional to get as much out of every encounter that I can. I have to make a habit of using the same intention and effort in my routine interactions, adding quality to my relationships and ultimately more quality to my life.

No matter where you are in the world, and how far away you are from loved ones, find time in your day to check in with someone and share your love for them. You might not have a lot of time, so be intentional with the time you do have. The effort is appreciated and felt, and the energy created in that moment continues to nourish the relationship after the moment has passed.

Acknowledge other people's feelings and emotions as reality—true as yours. This intentional form of communication highlights life's important messages: kindness, love, and happiness.

We are constantly communicating life's important messages with one another. Remember that happiness should be a constant message that we give and look for in others. I often think of my friends and family watching me play basketball and wonder what they see as I play. I have been told many stories about, as a fan, how stressful a game was or how nervous someone was while watching me play. After losses, I see the discouraging faces, and wonder: Has anyone ever watched me play and just noticed the smile on my face?

When happiness is valued higher than success, it is felt in the body and seen in a smile. It's talked about daily and highlighted in the way we look at everything we do in our lives. I love the game for the game itself, not just because I win or lose. We have to love life and appreciate all the moments for what they are, not what they are leading to, or the perceived success that may come after. Choose to highlight important ideals and direct your messages to individually define success and happiness as you see fit, encouraging this within all your relationships.

Be authentic:

Authenticity in relationships allows you to feel free, knowing that you can live up to who you are and what you bring to the table. Eliminate stress and uncertainty by not having to live up to an "idea" of who you are, guessing your role within each relationship. Internal struggle comes from trying to connect the person you "are" with an "idea" of what you're not. While others interpret, you remain constant. Let down your guard, your filters, and allow yourself to be seen for who you truly are, eliminating guess-filtering when it comes to defining your character and your qualities.

In 2020, the coronavirus was a large wake-up call to many people, in many ways. Friends and family used communication as a strength, providing the needed air to breath during troubled times. Actual phone calls replaced short abbreviated text messages. Video chats brought groups together, replacing random run-ins at a party. Looking forward, we can foresee that the world will go through many ups and downs, and we must always use the power of communication to bring connectivity and love, at all times.

Reach toward one another, using vulnerability as a strength, accepting all the qualities in other people, and ultimately accepting yourself for who you are. Communicate your thankfulness for the ones you love and choose kindness and respect toward the ones you don't know or don't yet understand.

I often remind myself to go back to the way Agathe and I used to communicate. I remind myself not to take any word for granted and realize that every moment has the potential to be special, and every person deserves to be treated with love.

REPROGRAMMING THE MIND

I used to believe that happiness was found in the way I "am," like if I can finally say, "I am successful," "I am rich," or "I am popular," then I'll be also able to say, "I am happy."

We're surrounded by a belief system that has left us feeling vulnerable and unable to sustain happiness on a consistent level, as life's luxuries and good fortune are not always within our control.

I don't believe that to be true anymore. The way I "am" will never leave me feeling authentically happy. Happiness is a mindset that we can control each and every day, despite any external influence.

Reprogramming the mind toward happiness begins with changing the structure of what happiness is, and how we experience it. As it stands now, "being happy" is a socially-warped definition of success, joy, and contentment. It confines us to a criterion where happiness is found in how you measure up to societal standards. "Feeling happy" is a restructured sense of happiness. Feeling happy stems from within and is an internal definition of what it means to be successful, joyous, and content.

When we talk about happiness, we must replace this idea of "being" with the experience of "feeling." This new approach means that we are the master of our own destiny—able to control what we feel and able to filter happiness into who we are and all that we see. Feeling happy means we get to reclaim our life by defining happiness for ourselves individually. There is no universally accepted definition of happiness, or any general understanding of what it feels like. It's up to us to define the feeling for ourselves.

Sure, you might feel a spark of short-lived happiness from things you possess, but sustainable happiness is found in the way we can consistently bring joy into all aspects of our lives. I try to find it around every corner, in everything I see, feel, and experience. When I don't see it there, I use my mind to restructure the things I see, in order to feel and amplify happiness where it already and always exists: within me.

For me, restructuring the mind to feel happiness comes down to a simple question:

Would I rather have all the desired things that people perceive as perfect to make me happy, or would I rather have an authentic and clear mind, with the ability to create love and happiness in all things?

When the power of your mind has the ability to create happiness in all environments and situations you encounter, then everything can be an authentic source of joy. A happier world already exists in your mind, and it is your privilege to unlock its power.

Happiness can become the foundation on which we base all of our pursuits, supporting us to experience life far beyond our possessions—anything that can be bought, sold, or lost. We have the ability to define our successes, and use happiness as our engine, propelling us to experience all that we can in this life.

Embark on a journey to redefine and reprogram how you experience the world, in order to see the happiness that is already in us and all around us. It starts with how we wake up each morning.

Reprogramming your morning intake:

In his 2014 TED talk, Tristan Harris, Google's former in-house ethicist and cofounder of the Center for Humane Technology, spoke about our addiction to technology. He said:

"When you wake up in the morning, you have certain goals for your life or for your kids; [technology] doesn't know any of those goals. It has one goal: to make you forget your goals and keep you watching as many YouTube videos as possible."

Begin each day by giving yourself a chance, asking one of life's most important questions: **How am I doing?** The internal should influence the external, not the other way around.

We check the weather and respond to it's daily forecast. We check the stock market, and react to its peaks and valleys. We check our phones, and are instantly influenced by the increasing volume of social media and information.

Before the world influences how you feel, find out how you actually feel. Find the areas in your life that you want to improve. Realize that you feel sad or upset, understanding why you feel the way you do.

There is a fight taking place every morning between external distractions and internal truth—a fight for the ability to influence our outlook on the day. According to reports from Common Sense Media, "American teenagers spend an average of nine hours per day with digital technology. Kids are spending more time with technology than they do at school or with their parents, making media the largest impact on their day."

And it's not just kids that are spending so much time with technology. Each morning, many of us begin our day by reaching for our phone or the remote control. We go external before we check in with the internal. Is your first "choice" each morning, without consideration, to welcome social influence into your mind, hearing the voices of the outside world before anything else? Are you going to base your day on how many texts or calls you received while you were sleeping or how many likes you got on your social media posts? Our initial focus is pulled toward the outside world, affecting the way we feel before even setting foot out of bed. And, it doesn't stop there. Every time we hear a notification, text, call, or update, we stop what we are doing and check our smart devices. What effect does this habit have on our daily outlook? What are we prioritizing?

Rethink your morning to prioritize a positive outlook based on your internal truth, not dictated by external influences. Your authenticity begins with your first thoughts and your first words.

For many, happiness is approached like a rating system from 1-10. From the moment we wake up, each new external thing entering or exiting increases or decreases our position on the scale. If we start our day at 1, it would take an exceptional amount of effort to reach 10 by the end of the day. Often, our day becomes filled with anxiety, thinking that we will never reach 10. Reprogramming our morning means that we don't start at 1; we can start at 10. Starting at 10 creates a higher level of sustainability, knowing that, even on a bad day filled with life's uncertainty taking us down from 10, we will still end up higher than having the same day but starting at 1. One alternative is reliant on the external to lift us up, while the other relies on the internal to create a successful foundation to our day.

The morning can provide an abrupt transition from the calm of sleep to the activity of your day. It can be difficult to transition between these two worlds. Are you filling that transition with negative external influences or with positivity? By reprogramming your morning, you can take control of the rest of your day.

Reprogramming adversity:

Chadwick Boseman, most well-known for his role in the film *Black Panther*, and top actor in Hollywood was diagnosed with stage three colon cancer in 2016. While undergoing treatment he continued working, volunteering, and inspiring. His passing in 2020 was a shock to many who never even knew of his diagnosis. How is it possible to face such intense adversity and remain so positive? For those of us who have never faced a life experience of this magnitude, what can we learn from Chadwick's last years?

I turned to medical researchers at John Hopkins to learn more about the effects of positivity on human health. The data is conclusive and inspiring:

- People with a family history of heart disease who also had a positive outlook were one-third less likely to have a heart attack or other cardiovascular event within five to 25 years than those with a more negative outlook.

- A positive attitude improves outcomes and life satisfaction across a spectrum of conditions—including traumatic brain injury, stroke, and brain tumors.

- Smiling—even fake smiling-reduces heart rate and blood pressure during stressful situations.

(**Source:** The Power of Positive Thinking, Johns Hopkins Medicine)

Life is full of adversity—difficulties that challenge our strength and determination. The more adversity, heartache, and sadness we experience, the less optimistic we are about happiness. We are tested by life and all its power.

But each day, we can find little ways to turn challenges into courage. We can create strength and see the positive outcomes beyond the adversity. Each day we can acknowledge the dark areas that hold us back and take steps to create a new path forward beyond the darkness.

Reprogramming adversity is rooted in optimism and positivity, thankfulness, and trust in yourself, the process, and the result. Reprogramming adversity is a powerful combination of positive filtering and positive soul communication, empowering you to control all the information you receive and to find happiness in all experiences.

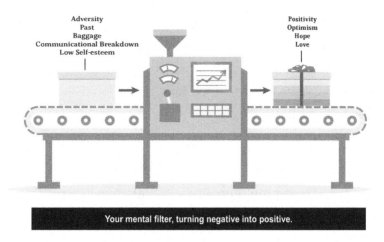

Adversity
Past
Baggage
Communicational Breakdown
Low Self-esteem

Positivity
Optimism
Hope
Love

Your mental filter, turning negative into positive.

We can no longer perpetuate the narrative that adversity is an unscalable mountain, that personal growth just stops at a certain point, and that "people don't change." We can always improve ourselves and our situation, starting with our mind. I think of Chadwick as he faced the toughest of adversity head on, literally embodying the life and character of a superhero, courageously fighting against the odds.

By reprogramming our mind, we arm ourselves with happiness before adversity hits. Just like trying to get out of quicksand without a branch, if you're battling against adversity without a rooted happiness, you'll struggle until it pulls you farther down. It is imperative to develop a mindset that will support you before, during, and after adverse times. As the medical research on positive outlooks proves, this mindset also helps to reduce the impact of life's stressors, better preparing you to avoid the quicksand altogether.

Our brain has the capability to restructure and pivot at any moment, even under extreme duress. My son, Léon, was born during the middle of the 2020 pandemic. From this, I learned that, even amidst a major global crisis, my heart, and what's important to me, has the ability to change in an instant. There was no feeling of confinement, as the concerns of the world took a backseat to the joy I felt being with my newborn son. Every day, we have the opportunity to create a better today and a better tomorrow, as long as we hold on to our reprogrammed perspective.

Become a person that can be challenged, that wants to be challenged. That can hear tough words, be faced with overwhelming odds. Be able to face a mountain, knowing with all your heart, you have the ability to climb it.

Redefine sacrifice:

Merriem Webster says:
"Destruction or surrender of something for the sake of something else"

We often believe that when we sacrifice ourselves, we become something less, a weakened version of who we are. On the contrary, to give yourself for something, or for someone, shows your humility and strength in becoming a better version of yourself or inspiring inspiration in others. When we sacrifice for the better of something or someone, we find purpose, we add meaning to our action. Without sacrifice, we lack the fullness of heart and the pride that goes into knowing that we are part of something bigger than ourselves. To understand sacrifice is to understand true ownership, true acceptance of who you are and the courage it took to get there.

Redefining darkness and pain:

"All the breath in your lungs is stronger than the tears
in your eyes."

—ARIZONA—

There is hidden beauty in sadness that we can see and appreciate; you cry because you have something to cry about, and you feel emotional pain because you have lost something or someone special to you. This means you had something or someone special to lose. It's a blessing to feel love and happiness to the point that sadness may be an end result.

Redefining darkness and pain is found in understanding that, whatever the world throws your way, you have the power inside of you to fight back stronger. It doesn't mean that all bad things are going to magically disappear. Instead, believe that at least one positive thing is possible amongst the bad. Just one. There is something to learn or something to take away from each situation that can have a positive impact on your life. Relieve yourself from some of the pain and stress that you feel in difficult moments, knowing that it takes time to truly understand the significance of what life throws at us—life can't be analyzed in a single moment. A closed door today might be the opening of a new door tomorrow—and maybe, just maybe, that's the one that is meant for you. Only time will tell.

In 2016, I lost one of my best friends. Each and every day since his passing, I have thought of my friend, Houston, and the incredible person he was. Every day, I choose to carry on his memory through thankfulness for our time together and perspective on what he taught me, rather than anger and frustration that he's gone. I do this by trying to embody his best characteristics and honoring all that I gained from my friendship with him. Tragedy should not be treated like a

New Year's resolution—moved on and forgotten by February. The pain of losing my friend is engrained into who I am, and Houston's memory is one of my biggest motivators and helps bring strength in becoming a better version of myself. Because of him, I value the quality of a life, the importance of now, and the thankfulness that, for some reason, I am alive, and I need to act accordingly.

You, too, can use each day to reprogram the adversity and pain in your life, in order to inspire yourself and those around you.

Imagine you are sitting in a very dark room. Suddenly, a door opens, letting in bright sunlight. You're amazed by how strong the light is, and take notice of its influence on the dark room. Now, imagine sitting in the same room, but this time, the room is partially lit by a lamp. The door opens, allowing in the same amount of light from the outside. The impact isn't as intense because of the light that already exists from the lamp. What does this show us? Bright light is most powerful and most impactful in the darkest of rooms and in the darkest of moments. If there was ever a time to consider your purpose, look no further, as there are many people in dark situations that need light.

Redefine darkness as an opportunity for light. Redefine pain as an opportunity to cherish life. Redefine heartache as an opportunity to feel the expanse of your love.

> "Darkness cannot drive out darkness, only light can do that. Hate cannot drive out hate, only love can do that."
>
> **—Martin Luther King Jr.—**

Reprogramming your bad mood:

What is a bad mood, anyway? Being in a bad mood is a combination of selfish thoughts and reacting to a situation that creates internal distress. I'm frustrated with something, I'm frustrated with someone, I'm tired and I don't want to do something. I feel like life is not going my way. There is a theme to most bad moods: they're all about "I" and "me."

Sometimes, bad moods don't even have a rational justification that you can point to for why you're feeling the way you are. Without taking control of the situation, we also project our bad moods onto other people, which isn't fair to anyone. What does reprogramming our mood look like? It starts with acknowledging that we're in a mood and by asking the important question: "Where do I go from here?"

Being in a bad mood is an opportunity to turn your focus and energy outward. Sometimes, to get "you" out of a bad mood, it can be as simple as not focusing on "you." Focus your mind on others and things that you can do to be a positive influence in the world around you. My day might not improve, but I can help improve someone else's.

The collective experience of Covid-19 gave us a lot of reasons to be in a bad mood, and also a lot of reasons to focus outward on others. For weeks on end, most of our communication with family and friends was over the phone, via text message, or FaceTime, as we were sheltering in place in our homes. I began to notice that, every time I connected with friends and family, I left the conversation with a good feeling, having shifted focus to things happening outside of my personal bubble. It takes courage in times of moodiness to give someone else the opportunity to improve your day. Fight that internal voice, telling you that you're "not in the mood" to make the call and connect with others.

If you find yourself in a bad mood, it's easy to stay in it, expecting something external to change, in order for your feeling to change. Being in a bad mood from time to time is understandable, but staying in a bad mood is unacceptable if you're not trying to inspire change within yourself. Take control of your situation. Don't become a victim of mood and circumstance. Empower yourself to decide where you want to go from here, thereby choosing the bad mood or a new alternative. This makes staying in a bad mood a choice instead of a reaction.

When you develop the habit of challenging and then reprogramming your moods, you realize that there are positive triggers all around to help you. It's difficult to stay in a bad mood when you surround yourself with people and things that bring you happiness. Don't overlook the power of simple things to reprogram your mood.

If you wait for the world to change your mood, you'll be waiting a long time. Take charge, initiate the right energy, the right environment, the right place to mentally and physically be yourself. Be proactive in reprogramming your bad mood.

Reprogramming "I'm tired":

As an athlete, I overuse the phrase "I'm tired." My wife has to listen to a broken record, as I constantly gripe: "My legs are tired; my body is sore; I just need to wind down; it's been a long day; got a long week ahead; was a long travel day," and the list goes on. While making plans, I often catch myself contemplating my decision based on if I have enough energy to do something or not. When I don't have the energy, it changes my outlook on the day, my motivation to do something, and the way I feel about what I'm doing.

We have become a generation of "tired" people, which is ironic when you think about how many things we do that don't even require us to leave our house. Life has become more and more convenient, yet we feel more worn down and tired.

"I'm tired" is more than a physical state; it's a mental state, a habit, and a self-fulfilling prophecy. The constant reminder of fatigue doesn't help give you more energy; instead, it makes it harder to do your daily tasks and connect with the world. Many of our frustrations and bad moods are a product of "tired." Small tasks seem bigger, smaller frustrations feel like more of a nuisance. Something as simple as taking out the trash might get on your nerves—you are frustrated to have to get up to do it, and frustrated at the people who asked you to do so. It's easier to zone out with social media and other external outlets that don't require us to do anything we don't want to do.

Have we gotten to the point that we are simply too tired for one another?

Notice how often you use some form of the phrase "I'm tired," and I bet you'll be surprised at how often you're defining yourself in this way. Ask yourself if you're actually as tired as you think you are. Has it become an auto response when people ask you how you're doing?

Say it out loud with me: "I'm *not* that tired!"

Don't wait for external motivation. I bet you're too tired to run a mile, but I guarantee you would jump off the couch and start running in your bare feet if you were offered a million dollars to do so. **Does your love for others, and yourself, provide enough motivation for you to be inspired to get up and find your happiness?** Does being a good parent give you the motivation to give your children the attention and love they deserve, even after a long day at work? The motivation to be there for a friend in need, even during a disagreement? The motivation to fight through adversity and anxiety, even when you feel defeated?

Define what gives you energy. Sometimes, you need to be energized by being around friends and family, filling your day with activities. Other times, you may need a restorative day by yourself. Reprogram your mind to understand that life is meant to be lived, not pass you by, as you get stuck in feeling "too tired" to feel alive.

Life is not full of things you "have to do," it is full of things that you "can do" and things you "get to do."

When you program your mind to think this way, you see life's opportunities instead of obligations. Change your vantage point in order to see that life is full of infinite possibilities. You are not small, a victim to the world, or unable to see where you fit in. Instead, you are bold in realizing the world has a lot to offer, and that you must decide what you want to take from it, what it is that your willing to fight for.

Redefining holes from your past:

No one is without a past. Perhaps you feel as if specific moments from the past have left irreparable "holes" in your present life. These "holes" might be symbolic of trauma, unrequited love, or an unrealized dream. To redefine the past is to understand that these holes no longer need to represent what is missing from the past, but instead they can symbolize available space to be filled with what you want for your future. Each hole can be filled, and you can choose what you fill it with.

There is no need to hide from, or feel ashamed of, the holes you have. When you identify each one—sometimes, the bigger the better— then you can go out into the world and find new replacements—new people, new hobbies, new avenues to start fresh and lead you to a happier self.

Forget the idea that your past should be perfect, should have been perfect, or will be perfect.

Life happens in growth, and we should feel fortunate to realize that. Feel free today, by letting go of the weight of yesterday.

Redefining judgement and insecurity:

My wife and I often try to find activities that we would enjoy doing together. A few years ago, I asked Agathe if she wanted to learn how to play golf so she could play with me and my friends. She responded by telling me that she needed lessons first, in order to be good enough to not hold the group back or feel ashamed of her play. She didn't want me or my friends to worry about her, making the game less enjoyable for us. The next time I was playing golf, Agathe did not join, and I mentioned her response to my friends. One of my friends laughed, saying that it didn't matter how bad or how good of a golfer Agathe is, or where she hit the ball. The truth is, everyone on the course is too preoccupied with their own ball, their own score, and what they look like with each swing. There will always be a better golfer on the course. So be it.

This response enlightened me and helped me to further understand insecurity and judgement in life. While we're so busy feeling anxious about the way we look or the way others might be perceiving us, the reality is that everyone else is too busy thinking the same thing.

Why do we feel judgement or insecurity about some perceived flaw or inadequacy? Why are we so insecure with our photos and what we see the mirror in selfie mode?

If everyone has flaws, why are we still calling them "flaws" at all?

No one is perfect. We should be celebrating our imperfections, just as we celebrate beauty and life. We should celebrate the things we're trying to improve, because they represent our ability to have our own mind, to have our own interests and tastes, to have our own strengths and weaknesses—our own uniqueness. The judgement you perceive from others is, in many cases, nonexistent, just manifested in your mind. **When you celebrate your imperfections, judgements hold no weight against the strength of your foundation.**

Redefining jealousy and envy:

When you look at a successful person, or someone who looks distinguished or wealthy, what are you really looking at? Are you envious of what they have, or are you envious of who they are?

Comparing yourself to another person is unhealthy because you will never be anyone other than yourself. However, you can adopt some of the qualities that you admire in them. Focus less energy on the person, less on the material things that indicate their success and more time on developing new skills and traits, adding qualities in yourself that you admire in someone else—patience, determination, courage, positivity, and resilience to name a few. When you focus on the qualities, you focus on attainable personal growth, what's tangible and real for you.

As you strive for more, keep perspective thankfulness, knowing that there is almost always someone in your life who would love to be where you are, wishing they had qualities that you have. To be an inspiration to others, all we need to do is be authentic about our best qualities, sharing our roadmap for success with others, in turn.

Redefining jealousy and envy means that we get to celebrate and encourage success in others, while identifying the aspects that we want to emulate in ourselves; just another mindful tactic to create happiness on our own terms, instead of the anxiety that comes through competition and comparison.

Reprogramming hate and ignorance:

As children, we learn about the world through the things we hear and see with naive, inexperienced eyes. As we grow older and more knowledgeable, it is our privilege and duty to understand that the world is full of different people, beliefs, and values. We have the choice, as human beings, to learn more about one another, in order to eliminate ignorance and hate. When we open our hearts and minds to learning beyond our comfort zone and our biases, we can become more aware of the different types of people in this incredible world we live in.

I have lived all around the world, and I have come to the conclusion that there is no reason for hate and ignorance toward anyone or anything. When we are insecure, we tend to become afraid of what we don't know or don't understand, and our fear manifests into hateful speech and ignorant thoughts. We have the tools to replace these damaging attitudes with compassion and love for one another. Reprogramming hate and ignorance gives us the conviction to become people who are more loving and more tolerant.

More than any time in history, we have the resources to learn about other peoples and cultures. We're already spending, on average, nine hours each day on our smart devices, looking at social media and surfing the internet. What if we spent just fifteen minutes proactively learning about a thing or a culture that we don't know about or that we're uncomfortable with? Push yourself out of your comfort zone; there's a whole world waiting just beyond. Only then can you truly test your character and authentic beliefs.

Are you going to see difference as something to hate, or as something to appreciate?

A reprogrammed mind will learn, before using judgement, to express kindness instead of hate, and will confront the bias that is within, and around, them. There is so much in the world we can learn, and when we choose not to be curious, we choose not to understand one another.

Reprogramming insecurity:

As I've experienced it, insecurity stems from destructive internal thoughts that we project onto our world and our loved ones. Insecurity exists because we relinquish valuable space and energy—space and energy that could be used for positivity and trust. Insecurity fills your mind with self-destructive doubts and fears, seeding feelings of inadequacy, like you're not good enough.

When you reprogram insecurity, you learn to fight away your own fear, limiting the space you allow negativity to have in your mind. This shift is not just in thought; it is experienced through your actions.

My desire is to see the world in a positive light; in order to make that a reality, I need to be positive. The thoughts that fill my mind create my reality. I don't want insecurity in my life, so I don't have insecure thoughts. I want to trust more, so I become someone other people can count on and trust. I want to live in an honest world, so I think honest thoughts and behave honestly. I want to live in a just world, so I value equality and inclusiveness and treat others with respect and dignity. My actions project a world that I will interpret as my truth, within my mind. Only then will I feel more secure.

As this positivity compounds in my mind, there is less and less space for negativity and insecurity to infiltrate. Even if external influences try to push me in other directions toward doubt, I choose to see the world through the security and trust of my own lens.

Reprogramming stress:

I'm often asked if I feel stressed before a game. The truth is, there are tens of thousands of fans out there who are already stressed enough for me, so why waste my moment to shine? Fans wear specific shirts, use numerous superstitions to help determine the outcome of the game. There is a stadium full of people who have emotionally invested in the game before I even step foot on the court. I want to make them proud, but I can't do that if I'm stressing.

I perform at my best when I realize that each game is just a part of the beauty of my journey, my story. I want to live out each moment, writing the script of my life, unencumbered by the stress of the outside world, while I learn to release the stress internally.

Perspective on your journey helps you to know that deadlines don't define you. External pressure may force you out of your comfort zone but doesn't change the content of your character. Stress can be used as a shock to the system, as you are lifted through motivation, saying it's time for action. Inspire those around you by your acceptance of stress and your courage to excel in all facets of your journey, and be thankful for all of your moments. I simply remind myself; Playing basketball is what I do, it's not who I am. **When I know who I am, I'm never stressed about what I do.**

Reprogramming fear of the unknown:

"By replacing fear of the unknown with curiosity, we open ourselves up to an infinite stream of possibility. We can let fear rule our lives, or we can become childlike with curiosity, pushing our boundaries, leaping out of our comfort zones, and accepting what life puts before us."

—Alan Watts—

Failure has a best friend: fear. Fearing potential unknown outcomes, or failure, leads to a lack of confidence in your actions, creating stress and anxiety in your mind.

When we fear the uncertainty of the unknown, our mind can become a hurdle, holding us back from reaching out for greater opportunities in the (equally unknown and uncertain) future. By the age of twenty-five, I'd say most people have already overcome about 1,000 stressful situations in their life. Yet, as soon as the 1,001th situation arises, we automatically become stressed again, filled with the anxiety that we may not overcome it, and that this specific situation is different from the rest.

Reprogram fear of the unknown by gaining confidence in the reality that you are much stronger than you give yourself credit for. As you live and breathe today, you already have climbed over seemingly unscalable mountains and overcome hurdles. You have made deadlines, fixed problems, and overcome adversities, making you stronger and more prepared to face whatever comes next. You have faced a pandemic, and you have chosen to fight back, taking control of your future. Replace fear with curiosity, helping to unlock your creativity and expression. Replace fear with action, enjoying your successes and learning from your failures.

Reprogramming dreams:

"You have to dream so big that you can't get an ego, 'cause you'll never fulfill all those dreams."

—Quincy Jones—

Whenever someone says that I dream too big, I know they don't dream big enough. Reprogramming dreams allows you to stretch your imagination, in order to take you further, imagining boundless experiences and futures that are bigger than human capabilities, beyond what anyone thinks is possible. You have an imagination and creativity—start applying them to your dreams.

A plane didn't just appear in the sky; it began as a dream to the Wright brothers, while other people laughed at the lunacy of the idea.

The blueprints for tomorrow are being created in the dreams of today.

Making a plan:

Unfortunately, with the combination of stress, adversity, and living in quarantine in 2020, we lost a lot of our ability to make plans for the future. How can we still dream big and create a future with so much unknown? Not being able to plan ahead, to see people or to travel, left many of us struggling to remain optimistic.

Redefine the way you plan, to include the many things you can control: plan time for soul communication, plan to call a friend, plan to share your gratitude for a loved one. For every one thing we can't plan for, there are endless things we can. 2020 inspired some companies to produce masks, change platforms, become mobile, and redefine the workplace in order to reinvent a newly designed future.

If the world is changing, then it's your privilege to be one of the people designing its change. Dare to be optimistic, dare to plan, and dare to dream, no matter the circumstance.

Reprogramming decision making:

Every decision you make comes from the result of a choice you have already made. If you choose a life of positivity you will redefine the way you make decisions and the stress and anxiety you feel around the choices you make. Each and every decision you will make comes with potential pros and cons, symbolizing the many routes in which your life may take course.

When I make choices I always focus on the things that I will add to my life, not the things I project could be taken away. The power of this "pre-decision" is seen in the spirit, action, and effort that comes after each choice is made.

Where your focus is, your mind will follow. Post-decision, you will either focus on the negative things, grass is greener type emotions, or be thankful for what each choice provides to your life.

Decisions are not about the lesser of two evils, instead, we should live in gratitude, shown through our effort and follow through, post decision.

Reprogramming time:

We stare at the clock and wait for school to finish, or stare at our calendar waiting for it to be Friday, excited about the weekend. Athletes wait for the season to start and the games to begin. We have been programmed to believe that some days will be far more exciting than others, disengaging or downright ignoring days that we consider "normal."

We spend a third of our daily twenty-four hours asleep and spend the rest of our day waiting for moments to begin or hoping that they will end.

Time is our most precious commodity. When we neglect the time we perceive as useless, we limit the potential for each and every day to be special, worthy of our attention, and inspirational. If we neglect 95% of our life waiting and anticipating the other 5%, we miss out on all of the potential happening right now, all around us.

Our days are filled with countless opportunities. Reprogramming time means we find purpose in more hours, creating higher value to more and more days in our life. I often smile thinking that, for so many people, today is a day they will never forget. Someone will meet a stranger who will one day become family to them. Someone might get their dream job, fall in love, or eat the best meal of their life. These are the moments we can't plan for, can't anticipate, but are life-changing nonetheless. Each morning, we make a choice to begin the right way, optimistically knowing that today might be the day. For what? Who knows . . . Let's be excited to find out. Make today a day to remember.

Redefining work:

The economic effects of the Covid-19 pandemic have impacted millions of jobs worldwide. For those of us who were furloughed or laid off, and for those of us who transitioned into working from home, we have all experienced change. Within these changes, we can find autonomy in redefining work for ourselves. We get to choose how we approach work today, as well as in the future. We can choose how we move forward, how we use this pause of uncertainty to redefine ourselves, and what we plan to do moving forward.

Perhaps you'll take your monthly salary and buy a new bike for your child or use your money to pay off an electric bill. It's important to keep perspective and focus on what your job creates for you and your life. Be specific in defining what each hour of your time spent at work can provide. Your time is valuable. The more specific you are with your intentions for the money you earn, the stronger your effort, commitment, and appreciation will be toward your work. I like to imagine that the hours I spend in practice and on the court during games will go toward providing shelter and food for my family, creating a better life for the ones I love. No matter the job, you, too, can redefine your work by the way you choose to spend your time and how you reward your effort.

We often feel frustration, thinking that our job is taking something away from us, taking our time, our effort, our sweat, and our life. Instead, we have to try to focus on the positive things that work gives us.

For those looking for a job, be specific and intentional with your time, each and every day. Apply, not just for a new job, but to begin a new way of life.

Reprogramming chaos:

While living in China, I was in awe of the style of driving I began to call "controlled chaos." It seemed that each intersection was a jumble of excitement and confusion, and to this day, I couldn't tell you which car, motorcycle, or person had the right-of-way. However, I also noticed that there weren't many accidents, not many cars pulled over on the side of the road or drivers exchanging heated words and insurance information. I was struck by the realization that such chaos actually resulted in less accidents than I was used to seeing in other countries with seemingly more controlled drivers.

I asked my Chinese teammates and managers about the driving, and they responded with a smile of acknowledgment, saying, "It's crazy, right?" What I realized was that these drivers were accustomed to the road, extremely prepared and more aware of their surroundings. Using quick reactions and reflexes they could avoid colliding with any other cars cutting them off at these messy intersections.

Just like an intersection in China, life is definitely filled with uncertainty, and we make choices at each intersection of life, in order to navigate through the chaos without incident. Are you prepared to encounter uncertainty and chaos? By redefining chaos, we prepare for whatever is coming our way before we encounter it. Redefine chaos by internally communicating outcomes, preparing yourself not for failure but for adapting to any deviation without losing sight of your destination. Remind yourself daily of your authenticity, your strengths, and work on weaknesses in order to prepare yourself for things to come. Realize that life has imperfections, and deviations are not always bad.

By redefining chaos, we no longer fall victim to our situation. Instead, we find opportunities to adapt, persevere, and realign with our goals.

Reprogramming ownership:

Living away from home for a long time, I have become pretty attached to my collection of favorite American movies. During my first couple of seasons overseas, I always carried my movies with me on an invaluable hard drive. I am a big film buff, and watching my collection of movies and TV shows helped me calm myself while traveling to new countries, riding on planes, and spending long hours in transit. Watching movies and shows even became part of my pregame ritual, and I used it to silence the noise around me before a game. This hard drive also contained personal photos and videos from growing up through college, as well as a valued collection of music that I had been accumulating for years. Writing this, I realize that this dates me as an older player, and it is hard for some people to realize life before Netflix, online music streaming, and completely accessible data.

One day, during preseason in Istanbul, I dropped the hard drive. It was broken beyond repair, and I was unable to save my files from inside. I felt incredible frustration that, with just one slip of my fingers, everything I stored and saved was gone. The loss of movies is far from life-shattering—very far—but it taught me two very important lessons: take ownership of your actions and protect the things you care about.

The first lesson I learned was to take ownership instead of blaming others: I'm the one who dropped it. Release the blame you put on other people, on the universe, or toward the obstacles themselves when you're experiencing some type of struggle. We often think, "Of course, this would happen to me. It's just that kind of day." Our tendency is to be quick to anger, thinking only of the things we have lost and the hardship it brings to our life. Whatever is happening to you, remember that you play a part in its happening. Taking ownership is not taking blame, but rather finding strength in honoring your involvement within your own life, in order to grow stronger through the encounter.

When you take ownership of something, it's important to constantly remind yourself that there was life before you owned it, and there will be life after. I was just as happy before I had all those movies downloaded, using them only to bring more happiness to my life, not being the reason for my happiness. This becomes more important when facing true adversity, knowing we can remain happy when anything is taken away from us, knowing that what we own doesn't make us who we are.

The second lesson I learned was to protect the things I care about. How well did I protect the hard drive and the movies, music, and photos it contained? Numerous times, I thought about buying a protective cover, to avoid this type of thing from happening. If I really cared about it, I should have made the effort to protect the contents I cherished so deeply. The things we put our time, effort, sweat, and tears into become the things that we care about and feel ownership toward. Our time and effort matter, as do the things our time and effort work toward.

How much care, time, and physical and emotional protection do you give to the important things in your life? What kind of protective cases do you have on the things you love? What kind of person are you before, and after, you lose things? Before and after you get metaphorically dropped? How easily do you crack, or are you indestructible?

Look into the areas in your life that are vulnerable to being cracked or broken. The more effort and care you put into protecting these things, the less susceptible they are to being broken.

Treat your relationships and cherished possessions with care, giving them protective cases for durability—and remember, a simple crack or fall doesn't define who you are or your ability to be happy.

Taking ownership of your life is asking yourself: "What's next?"

See how important this little question is, as it plays out through adversity and struggles in life. Taking ownership is deciding to take one of these two roads:

1. I have a problem . . . "What's next?" I'm angry because of it . . . "What's next?" Life is unfair . . . "What's next?" Look at where I am because of it.

2. I have a problem . . . "What's next?" I'm taking ownership of it . . . "What's next?" I'm going to work to fix it and make things better . . . "What's next?" Look at where I am because of my hard work.

These examples paint a very different picture, all stemming from asking the right question, taking ownership, and using your action to respond.

Reprogramming possessions:

The more possessions and things we have, the more potential we have for identity crisis and anxiety. Possessions are great, but often they can lead us to believe that happiness has a "look." Lose the idea that "this" is what happiness looks like or "that" is what unhappiness looks like. Life is far more complex than saying that being a rich person with the big house means happiness, or the person living on the street means unhappiness. We become accustomed to, and reliant on, the things we possess, making us feel as if we're dependent on those things for our own happiness. Your possessions should be working for you, not the other way around.

Often, I hear people speak about the difficulty of work, due to the fact that they must "work to the bone" in order to afford the things that they have. Some even neglect the things they love over the time it takes to maintain the things they have. The truth is, when we buy things, we don't just pay with money, as we begin to learn that the true cost of "things" is much greater. We pay for things with our time and our effort, ultimately with our life. Don't let the time you spend mostly consist of taking care of the things you possess.

Every time you buy something new, or upgrade what you have, tell yourself, "This new thing will not define my happiness. Possessions don't define me; I will define the value of each possession. Things may come and go, but I will remain me." Keep a constant perspective on what things cost, and realize that you are worth more than anything you can buy.

Reprograming perspective:

Life is not happening to you; it's happening for you, and because of you.

Reprogram your perspective to embrace each challenge life brings, like it has arrived for a reason—a positive reason. Challenges provide opportunities to act, to live, and to experience the entire spectrum of life. As the author of your own story, you have the ability to define the perspective you bring to each moment.

You don't need to go through something tragic to gain perspective, although tragedy can inspire a greater understanding of the incredible blessings life has to offer, as well as its fragility. Reprogramming perspective means not letting the same tragedy strike twice in the same way. Hold onto the lessons you learned the first time around, keeping them fresh in your mind. Perspective is something we must remember and maintain each day, not taking life for granted once you're back on your feet.

Redefining anticipation:

For Agathe, part of her happiness comes from keeping things fresh, through new experiences. She chooses to be excited and feel joyful anticipation towards all of life's events, large and small. Excitement and anticipation are a part of what I like to call "Christmas Theory."

Christmas is widely considered a joyful holiday. For those who don't celebrate Christmas, the same theory applies to the biggest holiday or annual tradition that you celebrate.

Growing up in my home, Christmas began each year on the morning after Thanksgiving with the sounds of Scottish bagpipes echoing throughout the house—a family tradition.

While playing basketball around the world, I have walked through incredible Christmas markets in Germany, France, and Latvia. Long before the actual day arrives, the streets are filled with people Christmas shopping, and it's easy to feel a change in the atmosphere. Anticipation grows as friends and family reach out with holiday greetings from near and far.

Some look forward to Christmas for the lights, singing, and gift giving. Others anticipate drinking eggnog, taking a vacation, or spending time with family. Some look forward to celebrating Christmas for the religious aspect, while others enjoy the spirit of the holiday season. I'll let you in on the secret of Christmas theory: the joy you feel isn't tied to a holiday—it always exists within you.

Christmas reminds us of the joy we feel when we experience anticipation. Consider all the things we do in preparation for our holidays, birthdays, or special moments. We spend hard earned money buying gifts and decorations, using our vacation days to fly or drive to different destinations. We prepare amazing meals, sharing food with the ones we love, giving people the time and effort they deserve. This is all made possible by your ability to create the feeling of Christmas, and we can adopt this type of feeling with more and more moments in our lives.

While living in Tel Aviv, I was inspired each Friday by the love and connectivity of Shabbat. Every Friday night, Jewish families gather around the table and share a meal, enjoying incredible food and conversation for hours on end. I was thrilled to be invited into many different homes, where I got to experience different family traditions. For each family, care and thoughtfulness went into the preparation of the food, the house, and inviting guests to share in the weekly feast. The joy of Shabbat is found in the weekly anticipation of bringing family and friends together, strengthening relationships, and sharing a nourishing meal. It's not a time that people *have* to spend together. It's a time that people *get* to spend together. I was surrounded by laughter, families sharing stories with one another and I rarely, if ever, saw a smart device deflecting attention from the moment.

The truth is, you really don't need a reason to celebrate; you can do it "just because." Prepare a meal for friends, plan a nice day at the park, or just prepare something special for no reason. Christmas theory lives inside you, so try to make the effort to plan and anticipate more happiness for your life.

Reprogramming winning and losing:

One of the biggest games I ever played was against UCLA during my senior year at Washington State University. With three seconds left on the clock, my team was two points down, and our coach called a timeout and drew up the last play of the game. I was to inbound the ball and find the open player who would make a shot to win the game. I passed it to an open teammate for the potential game-winning three-pointer. He took the shot, all of the Cougar fans held their breath, time stood still, and then the ball bounced off the rim. I heard the final horn and put my head down in defeat, feeling the pain of a tough loss.

After a postgame shower, I met up with my family and some friends who had traveled to be at the game. They tried, one by one, to console me. Or was it them that needed the consoling?

My dad looked at me and said, "What an awful game; I'm sorry." By that time, I had already let go of the painful loss and gained perspective about what had just transpired. I responded, "Awful . . . How come?" I went on to ask him, "Would it have been a good game if he had made the shot? A great game even?"

Truth be told, it really was an amazing game—well played by both teams and ending in dramatic fashion. If my team had made the last shot, and we had won, the game would have been the exact same, up until that last shot. The only difference would have been that the ball would have gone in. Fans, and players alike, mostly base their entire experience at the game on if that one ball goes in or not.

Of course, I am an extreme competitor who hates to lose, and I'm fully aware of the difference between winning and losing, but I also realize that sometimes it all comes down to one shot. The game itself wasn't a loss because only the scoreboard shows winning and losing. Happiness in your life is not based upon if you win or lose.

Just weeks later, I played in my final college home game, in the same arena, and with the same fans, except, this time, the outcome was a little different. This time, I made the final game-winning shot— the most memorable shot in my college career. The fans rushed the court, and my family and friends celebrated with me all night long.

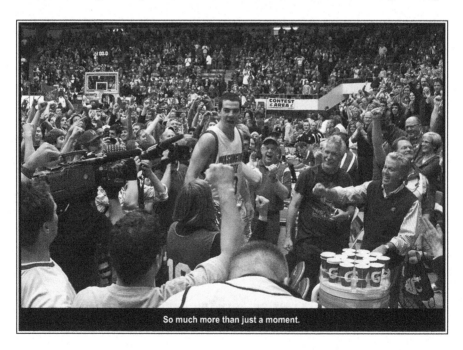

So much more than just a moment.

For me and my team, it was in the process—the ups and downs of our seasons together—that made that last shot so special. It was the combination of all the missed shots and bad games. It was the product of all the rehab and pain I went through during the season leading up to that last home game. It was because of all my teammates and the relationships I built—as strangers turned into a brotherhood. My passion roared as I celebrated the entire process leading up to the moment, a process that far exceeded that one single shot.

But I made the game-winning shot, so that's why I'm happy, right?

Basketball, like life, comes at us fast. Just two weeks after this photo was taken was my last game in a college uniform. My college career ended with a loss in the postseason tournament. I walked into the locker room and took off my WSU jersey for the last time. In Division 1 basketball, there are only two champions—one NCAA and one NIT—while every other team ends their season with a loss. Do only the two championship teams have the right to celebrate? Do only those players get to be appreciative of the season?

When we lost that night, I experienced uncontrollable tears—a mix of emotions, including sadness, happiness, relief, and thankfulness. Once again, I was emotional because of the process. I was happy to be part of heart-breaking losses, as well as incredible wins. I felt truly thankful to be able to experience it at all—thankful for my scholarship, for my coach putting me in the game, for my talent as an athlete, for my parents' amazing job raising me and encouraging my passion, and for my brother shooting hoops in the backyard, schooling me over and over again, pushing me to be better and better.

My career has been a journey of blessings, filled with countless wins and countless losses. No scoreboard defines me because I define success in the process. It is defined through the fullness of my heart, and the passion I bring every step of the way.

Redefining confidence:

Agathe and I decided together that, if I was going to continue my dream as an athlete, she would support me by living with me in different countries. As we constantly change our location, it's difficult for her to work or create a career for herself, and she has gone from taking care of me, being pregnant, becoming a mom, to taking care of our growing family. I like to think that she has to take care of three kids—me included.

In seemingly innocent conversations with friends and strangers alike, I began to notice questions seeded with judgment of Agathe's choices. I think many stay-at-home parents, and other professions, experience the same type of inquiries from others.

"So, what do you do?" people would ask.

"I'm a stay-at-home mom, and I support my husband," Agathe would respond.

"Is that all?"
"You don't work?"
"What do you do all day?"

There are so many inflection points like this in our day. Whether it's about being a stay-at-home mom or thinking you must defend who you are and what you do. These questions carry big weight, in terms of the way we shape our feelings about ourselves. A lack of confidence in situations like these leads to doubt—doubt in the person you currently are, doubt in your past decisions that got you here, and doubt toward what's to come next.

Can you hear the lack of confidence and fear in these responses?

"Ya, it's just for now."
"I would rather be working."
"I have to do what I have to do."

Fear of judgment—external and internal—is very real in these moments, as we want to believe that we are living our best life, not missing out on something better. We turn to social media and compare ourselves to what other people are doing, making it hard to water our own grass, as we envy the grass on the other side. This rabbit hole of insecurity limits your courage to think, speak, and act with confidence.

Or, moments like these can be a catalyst for our confidence to speak our authentic truth.

"I feel so lucky and blessed."
"I love the time that I spend with my family, and I feel like this is right where I want to be in my life right now."
"There are plenty of things that keep me active as I try to learn and grow each day."
"I may get a job or try something new in the future, but I'm thankful now, excited to see what life will bring my way."

Can you hear the confidence in these answers?

Your conviction leaves little room for rebuttal. Speaking with confidence doesn't mean you think your situation is perfect; it conveys how your situation brings you strength, not weakness.

When you have confidence in your decisions, who can argue?

Deep self-awareness gives you the answer before the question is even asked. I am happy with who I am, and there is always room to inspire more for tomorrow.

Reprogramming value:

"Do not educate your children to be rich. Educate them to be
happy, so when they grow up, they will know the value of things,
not the price."

—Victor Hugo—

Think of going to a party where everyone is wearing a name tag. However, instead of just their name, each person has also written a list of things they need in order to be happy.

In this situation, the people wearing the name tags are identifying the cost of the things that bring them happiness. These people aren't able to focus on their relationships—the actual people there at the party—because they've narrowed the conversation of what makes them happy from "how" and "why" down to "how much."

By reprogramming value—hopefully starting from a young age and listening to Victor Hugo—our name tags, values, and the way we identify ourselves will be completely aligned.

Now, with the things we want being identified by the value they will bring to us instead of the cost, we are able to be present, and talk about the things that matter—finally able to connect to one another and share our lives in a meaningful way. These are the things that bring us closer together, values that last, ideals that are meaningfully shared. These ideals highlight the journey, the 95%, not just the destination.

Redefining "first looks":

As I walk into a room, I wonder what people see when they first look at me, what they initially think. I wonder how many people would like me without knowing me, and more interestingly, how many people wouldn't like me, even if they didn't know a thing about me.

We are filled with preconceived notions that impact what we see. Our personal histories, how we were raised, what we were taught, and how our thoughts have evolved over time, shape our story and shape our mind to see the world in our own unique way.

We have a tendency, as a society, to make determinations and form opinions based on "first looks." But, is that really fair or accurate? Can you assess someone's values just from one look? Can you know their heart, their hopes, and dreams?

Redefining first looks means we are not judging books by their cover, and instead we are open to the possibility that first encounters can turn into life-long relationships, deep conversations, and forever love. If we wrote off all of our first looks because of judgment we would miss out on all of this. So, what should we be looking for?

Reprogramming beauty:

Imagine being in a room and hearing that the most beautiful person in the world is about to walk in. What do you expect? Supermodel looks? Do you anticipate seeing kindness, and being inspired through positivity?

Do you have the same reaction toward external beauty when you know the content of the interior? What is true beauty?

I believe that your true beauty is found in the spirit, attitude, and presence you bring with you—in all that you do. If you know people to be unkind, you don't see them as being beautiful in the full sense of the word. Know that when you put your internal beauty on display, this is what is truly seen and felt when you walk into a room and what is lasting and inspiring to those you meet long after you leave.

Put your love, positivity, and kindness constantly on display, making you more beautiful each day.

Reprogramming your "type":

"What's your type?" We've all heard this question from friends eager to find out what "type" of person we are attracted to. Perhaps your type is someone with a nice smile, a good job, and lots of friends. Or, perhaps you subscribe to an old school type: tall, dark, and handsome.

When you describe your type, how often do you include attributes and values like "happiness" or "joy" in your list? Going further, are you thinking about the type of partner you want to be for someone else? What attributes and values do you bring to the table that influence what you look for in someone else?

Reprogramming your type means that you restructure what you're looking for in someone else to be more closely aligned to your authentic self, thereby restructuring the value you place on each quality.

Focusing on finding a partner with the surface features we think we like has not led to reliable happiness, yet this is what our eyes are programmed to desire. By reprogramming our type—holding happiness at the top of our pyramid—we restructure what beauty and attraction means to us, as well.

So, what are you really looking for in a partner? This is your opportunity to reevaluate the attributes and values that truly make up your type.

Redefining identity:

Not being a fluent French speaker, I spent the first couple of years visiting France with Agathe, barely able to speak with her family and friends. I realized that who I was during these visits was a translated, then interpreted, version of myself. I was who my wife said I was, and what her family interpreted me to be, after processing Agathe's translation. With my identity altered and personality stripped, I felt vulnerable to false representation.

Each year, my French improves, and I am able to speak more and more confidently with Agathe's family and friends, sharing more of my authentic personality in each encounter. My job is to continue to shine in my authenticity, so the world has the best chance to see me for who I truly am, no matter their interpretation. Realize that who you are is a matter of who the audience is, and how they interpret what they see and hear. You can only control what you can control, so make sure your authentic self is on display as much as possible.

Redefining perfection:

One night in China, I was finishing up with a team practice and glanced over to an adjacent court, where I saw a kid working on some drills with his dad. Right away, I noticed some minor adjustments I could help him with, so I felt the urge to walk over and give him some advice. While dribbling the ball, he was hunched over, staring down at the ball and not able to see the court or focus on the basket. I encouraged him to keep his head up and eyes forward while dribbling, in order to see where he was going. He looked at me and said, "Okay." He tried the exercise again, and like the first time, his head remained down. I stopped him again and asked him why he didn't have his head up, thinking that maybe he didn't understand what I was trying to teach him.

He said, "If I keep my head up, I can't see the ball. If I can't see the ball, then I can't do the drill perfectly." He continued by saying, "If I can't see the ball, I'm going to make a mistake."

I laughed a little, thinking about the countless mistakes I have made in all the drills I have done over the last thirty years of playing basketball. I asked him to tell me who his favorite NBA player was, and I confided in him that even the best NBA players make mistakes in almost every game.

We are programmed to aim for perfection when our focus should be on improvement. Each day, I focus on becoming a better basketball player, not a perfect basketball player. Redefining perfection allows us space to structure our mind toward daily applications and personal effort. Aim for perfection and we end up making mistakes, leading to frustration. Aim for improvement, and we end up with progress, one step closer to where we want to be.

Redefining appreciation:

Typically, when I come home from work, I arrive not just at a house, but at a home. My wife creates this home for us through her presence and her contributions. Agathe appreciates living in a beautiful place that we can both be proud of. She once mentioned to me, I always want to live in a cozy and tidy home, even if it were just me living here."

Agathe feels personal satisfaction and pride in the way the house looks, regardless of the feedback she may or may not get from me. This carries over to the underappreciated, and always overlooked, role of being a partner and a parent.

While we might not always hear words of affirmation or reassurance that the work we are doing is being noticed and appreciated from external sources, we have the choice to appreciate ourselves. When you learn to appreciate yourself—your effort and your contributions—you find contentment and reassurance from within.

Most of our daily efforts go unnoticed, making it easy to feel undervalued and underappreciated. But we have the ability to choose how much we are appreciated and why we do what we do.

The point of this is to ask yourself: What is the goal in doing the things you do? Do you find self-satisfaction in your daily efforts, or are you doing them to receive some sort of recognition for your contribution?

I often think about my career and ask myself if I would still be playing if I felt that I was being underappreciated as a player? I can't control the way others show appreciation, but I know my self-worth and choose to appreciate my effort, my passion, and my drive. If you need confirmation in your effort, then you are internally undervaluing yourself and your work. Never doubt your contribution when you give the world a piece of who you are.

Be a person who appreciates validation but doesn't require it to maintain the same level of happiness.

Redefining scope:

For the first six months after my daughter, Joy, was born, Agathe and I stayed awake many nights, listening to her breath, as she experienced respiratory issues, colic, and two bad cases of bronchitis. In the mornings, we would again listen attentively, hearing that her breathing had not gotten better, and imagined the long and arduous day ahead. We felt scared for our newborn baby, and we were both exhausted from many sleepless nights. Some mornings, we felt like our only option was to forfeit the day, as the only thing that mattered to us was hoping for her to feel better "tomorrow." It's not easy to compartmentalize or to see past something so critical as the health of your own child. In moments like this, your scope is narrowed, and the world can feel very small.

Even in moments like this, we can widen our lens, let in thankfulness, and be aware of the broader world around us. We need to create inspiration and motivation, especially in times that can leave you feeling pessimistic. I know that my wife and I certainly did.

Redefining scope means setting aside just a piece of your mind—if only a small percentage—for openness and optimism that will allow in the positive external creativity that the world has to offer. Possibilities for growth and happiness only come when we remain open to them.

Think about all the random encounters that ended with incredible stories. Married couples, lottery winners, incredible friendships, and other amazing things that began when someone took a chance, opened their door, and widened their scope. Redefining scope means you don't close your mind to the potential of each day and, instead, give each hour the optimism it deserves.

Reprogramming forgiveness:

To forgive is to see the humanity of yourself portrayed in someone else—to realize the importance of connectivity, understanding that we all share the characteristic of not being perfect. We are all deserving of love over judgment, compassion over anger. Forgiving someone else is forgiving your own flaws, forgiving your own mistakes, and accepting yourself.

Redefining thankfulness:

Some people think that thankfulness stems from having many mazing things to be thankful for, or one grand reason to be thankful. And sure, those instances of intense gratitude are worth noticing and appreciating. But consistent thankfulness—the kind you can experience each and every day—steps from internal perspective. Constant thankfulness doesn't actually require anything to be thankful for.

In 2016, I was midway through my season playing in Russia, when I hurt my knee and spent some time on crutches. This wasn't the most ideal place or time to be hurt, as Russia is not known for its mild winters. I was facing eight to ten weeks of rehabilitation before I would be able to be back on the court. I remember seeing my phone flooded with texts and calls, as family and friends sent their condolences for my setback. To me, this was a minor setback—the kind that unfortunately becomes commonplace for athletes.

But, it wasn't easy. I couldn't walk for the first month after my injury. Our bedroom was up a long flight of stairs, which led to very humbling walks, as Agathe waited patiently and helped me navigate each step.

I was unable to play the game I love. I was living in snow-covered Russia, away from friends and family. What was there to be thankful for?

A few weeks later, I was able to get off crutches and start walking, but the pain was tremendous. Why should I be thankful now? The blood rushed to my knee and ankle every time I stood up, sending shooting pains down my body.

I began to walk around more and even began to do some small non-running workouts. Sharp pains shot through my body. I was cussing like a sailor in frustration that I couldn't do anything the way I used to. Am I thankful yet?

Workouts got more intense, and I started to run but couldn't yet play. I watched countless games from the sidelines, unable to help my team, not being on the court for my teammates through important wins and losses. Am I thankful yet?

I started to practice with the team, but I felt a step behind. If I could just play the way I knew how, I'd be happy. Am I thankful?

I healed and got back on the court. My minutes have declined, and I don't play as much. I don't play as well, either, and don't move as fast. Am I thankful?

Criticism pours in from the outside world as my statistics drop. I'm just not the player I know I can be. So, why should I be thankful?

How many chances did I have to be upset or frustrated? How many opportunities did I have to be thankful?

Each step of the way, I was not where I wanted to be, but the truth is that, with each step, I was exactly where I was hoping to be, when I was one step behind.

As soon as that injury happened, I had a choice: to be frustrated and focus on the injury or choose a perspective of thankfulness. I chose to work on my soul communication like I had discovered in college, visualizing my return and trying to stay positive. Through this injury, I evolved even more in my realization that thankfulness can become a solution to recovery, and a way of life.

So, here's what really happened when I approached my injury with thankfulness. When I received the results, I was thankful that the injury wasn't worse, and I knew I could handle it because I would focus on my effort and improvement, knowing I have overcome adversity before. I was thankful that my wife was there to support me and laugh as my crutches were sliding on the ice. When I was on crutches, I looked forward to taking my first steps without them, and looked forward to the prospect of getting back to practicing with my team. Each day, I had the opportunity to be thankful for being exactly where I was—a step further in my healing than I was the day before.

Even while I was healing, I was actually thankful for my injury, as it gave me the opportunity to learn about the value of my daily attitude toward the challenges I face. It gave me a newly-awakened desire to play basketball and a new drive to be even better than I was before, feeling the loss of being without the sport I love. Trials and tribulations have the ability to show you where you stand, encouraging a thankfulness for who you are.

We often let daily experiences go by unnoticed, when we could be experiencing thankfulness for them. I'm thankful anytime I don't feel sick or in pain. Thankful for the days I get to work and have a job. Thankful for the friends I have and the ability to make my own choices. Thankful to live in a time where I can express my voice and create my world.

The truth is, we all have so much to be thankful for each day, once we reprogram thankfulness. Feel strong about who you are and what your current situation is, while cherishing both in the moment. Simply being present and active in trying to find our own happiness is something to be thankful for, and something not to take for granted. There is never a time to stop being thankful—to live in "endless thankfulness."

Redefining the 4th quarter:

I am a very confident person when I play basketball. My opponent might be better than me, faster than me, or stronger than me, but not today, not this game. None of that matters when the game is on the line because I know who I am, my capabilities, and I want to take the last shot, no matter who's guarding me. When my moment comes, I will be more than ready for it because I work hard, and I live for these moments.

In these moments, when it matters most, when my team, or family, or wife, or babies, or friends need me, all they have to do is say the word, and I will be there. We have to understand that our life is ours, and it is the only one we get. We have the power to hit the pause button at any moment in life, regain strength, and redirect our courage where it matters most. We create the important moments, and we can choose to step up and not shy away when they present themselves.

When I told the story about my most memorable game—the winning shot as a collegiate athlete—what I didn't mention is that this shot came after I had missed ten or more shots in a row leading up to it. My 4th quarter wasn't defined by those missed shots, or even by the one game-winning shot itself. My moment was defined by my presence on the court, my desire to want the ball, and my confindence to know that my shot was going in.

Redefining the 4th quarter means that you show up when you're needed most—you rise to the challenge, even when, and especially when, the going gets tough. The 4th quarter is not the moment to back down, lose confidence, or give up. The 4th quarter is your time to shine.

Reprogramming expectations:

Expectations have a funny way of fooling the mind into thinking that things are not okay now, but they'll be better in the future. Expectations plant seeds of entitlement, causing us to believe we somehow deserve the perfect outcome we've designed in our heads. Expectations lead to anxiety, confusing us into thinking that, if our experience doesn't match our expectations, we've done something wrong.

There is a fundamental difference between setting goals for yourself and setting expectations. Goals create a desire to achieve and stimulate a work ethic.

Goals help you focus on the process, while expectations focus solely on the outcome.

I have had the goal of becoming a professional athlete since I was ten years old. From a young age, people have been trying to manage my expectations, preparing me to "not make it." I can remember countless conversations in which friends, teachers, and academic advisors openly shared that they did not believe I could reach my expected outcomes. Posted on the wall of my counselor's room in high school, there was a page of statistics, highlighting the unlikelihood of a high-schooler becoming a Division 1 athlete. The stats went on to show the even smaller percentage of young athletes who actually make a profession out of their sport.

As a teenager, I hated these charts and all the discussions that came with them. I was told I shouldn't put "all of my eggs into one basket," that I should focus on academics, that I should prepare to have a backup plan. Wait, if I can't dream big, then what am I really telling my heart, soul, and mind? Why inhibit your dreams, stunt your growth, or let yourself be persuaded to give up on your dreams before fighting to achieve them?

I'd say that 99% of the people in my life, when I was growing up, would ask me, "What are you going to do when basketball doesn't work out?"

What everyone failed to understand is that I have never felt entitled. I have never had expectations to become a pro athlete. It was my passion and my goal.

I answered all nay-sayers by increasing my passion for the game, improving the way I play basketball, and improving the way I lived my life. I chose to believe in my own dreams and my own capabilities, surrounding myself with people who supported me and my goals. My dream remained my main focus while supplementing my scope with other hobbies that create a well-rounded balance to who

I am. I did not lose my dream by losing my focus. I did not expect anything, yet I worked for everything.

There is a structural difference in our minds between setting expectations for things to work out and courageously setting goals to give them the best shot at working out. Are you focused on creating your backup plan and managing your expectations, or are you working toward your goals, inspiring a hunger to achieve them?

Redefining obligations:

Obligation can sound like a scary word. Being obligated to something or someone can sound controlling, confining, or limiting. When you feel obligated to do things you don't want to, you start feeling the weight of the world controlling who you are. But the truth is that many of our obligations are things that we choose to bring into our lives, like having a job or a partner, taking care of a sick relative, or making plans to see friends. And that's the crux: *you* should be the one defining your obligations.

You may not be able to control what your job is or who your boss is, but you can control the conversation you have at your job, or the way you interpret your boss, the way you define the work you do and its influence on your life. You may have an obligation to make money, but you can reprogram this obligation to see how it creates happiness through the things you are able to provide.

When you project positivity from your obligations, they can be transformative for you and for others. Whatever you've obligated yourself to do, you can be impactful while doing it.

Reprograming nonbelievers:

In life, some people will believe in you and others won't. Know this: no matter what side they're on, everyone in your life can provide motivation and inspiration for you to become better and stronger. Our motivation is strongest when it is not spiteful, but is, in fact, thankful—thankful for everyone who supports you and believes in your journey, and thankful for the critics and nonbelievers who remind you that hard work is a choice; and it's not for everyone. Ultimately, they all play a role in your success and help shape your character.

Reprogramming truth:

Our minds have been programmed, from a young age, to think that what we believe is true, and what is true is fact. If what we believe is true, then anything that we don't believe in is fair game to be viewed as controversial or even false.

We have put up boundaries our entire lives without knowing it, separating and arguing, our truth vs. your truth. Our country vs. your country. Our ideas vs. your ideas.

Here's the real truth: what we believe to be true may not be true for everyone else.

The day before I got married, I was enlightened by a very humbling truth. I was being a controlling person. In fact, I *was* a controlling person, had been for a long time, just not in my eyes. I will be the first to tell you that I'm still far from perfect, but leading up to the wedding, it became pretty obvious that I needed to work on my controlling tendencies.

A New 20/20 Vision

It's so difficult to identify the weaknesses within ourselves, yet so easy to find them in others. We justify who we are and what we do with our internal thoughts. We believe we are good people on the inside, so we must be showing that on the outside.

The lightbulb turned on in my brain as I walked down the aisle during the wedding rehearsal. I finally understood what Agathe had been trying to explain for years—most fervently in the months of wedding planning. We were interpreting my actions, my truth, in two very different ways. There were two truths: hers and mine.

Most people will not feel comfortable enough to let you know if there are things for you to work on or ways in which you can improve, if that means you need to change something about yourself. Then, we are most often not comfortable enough to receive the message as a potential positive for change, thinking that we couldn't possibly be the problem. The change we need to make is not becoming inauthentic and different; it's knowing that everyone is entitled to, and has, their own truth.

As I approached the alter, I realized that, what she experienced as being "controlling," I had always seen as being "helpful, informative, protective, and caring."

Suddenly, I understood. I felt I was protecting Agathe from harm, letting her know which street to take, in order to avoid traffic, or suggesting that it would be wise to bring a sweatshirt to the movie theater because it gets cold in there. She felt I was just telling her what to do. In my mind, I was being loving and helpful, as my intentions were pure, and if she could read my mind, she would know

—122—

how loving my intent was. Well, she didn't see it that way, and I'm sure many would agree with her. To her, many times, it just felt like I was telling her what to do, trying to control the situation, or implementing my belief system.

I spent the entire wedding rehearsal being more aware of myself and my helpful/controlling thoughts, quieting the urge for me to speak up on behalf of other people.

So, who's experience was the true experience? Who was right?

Well, in a way, we were both right. However, finding a winner or placing blame didn't matter. It's not about being right; it's about understanding our individual "truths" and how to accept them in one another. Agathe and I interpret the world in different ways, and her truth is just as valid and important to me as mine.

If I try to inspire happiness in her, then I need to understand the way she receives love and what's best for her, not me. I choose to remain my authentic self, and may even have the same thoughts, but I evolve in my understanding, in order to use different words and different action, or inaction, to honor both of our truths.

Redefining truth is about understanding that we all have different perspectives and ideas, and we can acknowledge and appreciate others' truths just as much as our own. Don't be frustrated that people don't understand you, finding conflict through daily interactions. Understand there is a free and authentic person on the other side of whatever communication you take part in.

Reprogram preferences:

Growing up, I remember seeing Nike commercials that made me want to "be like Mike." I definitely wanted to be a basketball star like Michael Jordan, so I drank Gatorade and wore Nikes, just like him. I came to Europe and found out that soccer was the top sport, and Adidas the top preferred brand among pro soccer players.

While deciding which athletic brand you prefer is a pretty harmless preference, other choices can be much more controversial.

Preference is simple: we choose to like something more than something else. Choosing a side, however, is an acknowledgment that there is a competition, a winner and a loser. The risk comes in the way we treat one another and the potential problems that arise within competition. Choosing a "side" in politics, for example, creates a situation of anxiety among friends and family, creating division and even enemies. Our preferences do not mean we need to choose sides. Having a preference just means that we have chosen what we prefer, not that the alternative is wrong. Again, we realize that there is more than one truth, more than one way of thinking, and we should celebrate our preferences as valued differences, not threatening competition.

Reprogramming small talk:

Years ago, I was helping Agathe learn some conversational sayings in English. We got on the subject of small talk, and I tried to explain some of the most common responses for day-to-day questions: "Not bad," "Pretty good," "Not much, same old thing," "I can't complain," or "Ah, you know . . ."

Small talk is a breeding ground for complacency, mediocrity, and auto-responses that define our lives—if we let it. The words we use, and the responses we give, become extremely repetitive and ingrained in our minds.

"Not bad, pretty good, can't complain."

These are the words that influence our thoughts and lay the foundation of our interpretation of life. If you want to live a "pretty good" life, then give "pretty good" answers, and ask "pretty good" questions. If you desire something more, then your words and optimism for life should reflect your desire.

Redefine small talk as an opportunity to stimulate your life through questions and responses filled with words of excitement. Turn the question, "How are you?" into "I heard things are going great in school, and you got an A on that science project—that's amazing! What was the project about?" You'll see answers and engagement far beyond the one-word answers like "fine" or "good" that we're accustomed to. By redefining small talk, you open doors to conversations and insights that were always there.

If you want to live an amazing life, then you can't accept "whatever" or "pretty good" as your auto-response. Challenge yourself to make better small talk—challenge yourself to a better life.

Redefining "can't" to "can":

I love hearing people say they can't do something: "I can't run a marathon," "I can't cook," "I can't play guitar." I love hearing these comments because then I get to ask, "Well, have you tried?"

Redefining "can't" to "can" begins with an approach, then continues with your effort and your attitude while doing it. Not many people have succeeded in doing something if they start by saying they can't do it. Encourage yourself to be a person who only uses the word "can't" after trial an error, and trial again. Never be your own first obstacle.

Redefining your odds (group happiness):

If we truly are invested in our relationships—caring for each other as we care for ourselves—our chances to achieve sustainable happiness multiplies. Think of the closest people you have in your life. Let's say there are five people in this group.

Your group of five gives you a five-times-better chance each day of being happy because they are sharing in your happiness with you, and you are sharing in their happiness, too.

If you view your happiness as "personal" or "individual" happiness, then you're missing the big picture. Our happiness belongs to us just as much as it belongs to our loved ones—our support system, our fan club. We can all share in joy and happiness together. Vice-versa, we invest so deeply in others' happiness, that their happiness becomes ours, as well.

Your group will provide a safety net for any falls but, more importantly, create a ladder to higher success and more sustainable happiness. Each day gives you five opportunities to share news of excitement, optimism, and encouragement. Five chances to feel success, love, and share it with one another.

Group happiness is our new model toward sustainable happiness. It is the answer we have been looking for, defining how we will change the way we treat one another in our new vision for the world.

Reprogramming your bedtime intake:

Before putting Joy to sleep, Agathe and I read stories with her. We wind down from the day and cuddle up together, transitioning from the busy day to a calm night. For Joy, this transition period is critical to a good night's rest. As adults, are we so different? I don't think so.

Just like a toddler, we need to be aware of our final thoughts before sleep. Positivity and optimism for the future need to be the way we start and the way we end each day. Control the way you fall asleep, the thoughts that put you to bed, ultimately setting the stage for tomorrow.

Reprogramming future happiness:

When we're together, my dad and I like to go to the movie theater. Before the movie starts, we watch the trailers. After watching each one, my dad turns to me, letting me know which movies he is excited about and which ones he isn't interesting in seeing. In fact, the whole theater is probably aware of his preferences, as he finds it hard to not show his excitement for an upcoming movie.

With most things in life, just like movie trailers, we decide if we like something or not before we have it, before we see it, or before we feel it. Part of knowing what you love is feeling the anticipation of having it. We get excited about "what's to come," creating a hypo-thetical reality before truly living it out. Our minds are busy today interpreting and envisioning our future for tomorrow. This concept of promotional happiness poses one of the most critical and influential questions you can ask:

Are you promoting future happiness for yourself?

Promoting future happiness helps us envision a life that is motivational, exciting, and worth living for—worth being optimistic about. We must be the best advertiser, the best salesperson, and the best motivational speaker when we look at our own life, creating joy and happiness for what's to come.

In his TED talk, Harvard psychologist Dan Gilbert teaches that synthetic happiness and real happiness are very similar experiences. His studies show that happiness is just as attainable and just as real when you don't get exactly what you want. In fact, it can be even better.

Wait, so even if your future doesn't turn out like you had initially imagined, the amount of happiness you experience can be equal? This has to be the best news ever. This is the answer to anxiety, to nerves, and worry. This is the root of our confidence and optimism. I can set goals, work to achieve them, and potentially be just as happy, or more, if I don't get what I want.

When I sign a contract, I envision a dream season, while remaining open to whatever comes my way. I envision playing at my best, having the best situation with teammates, and loving the new city my family and I will be living in. I envision that something amazing will come from my decision. I'm open to the ways that my new team will challenge me, and confident in my ability to exceed expectation and work each day to become better. I sell myself on everything in life. I find a reason that the next meal will be amazing, the next game will be my most memorable, and the day ahead of me could be full of surprises and positivity. Why do I do this? Because I can, because it's my choice, and because it is my truth—everything in the future can be filled with happiness.

Imagine going to a party where everyone in attendance is only wearing blue clothes. During the party, you see someone walking in wearing all red. Their presence would stand out, and make it easy to see that something doesn't fit with its surroundings. This is the same atmosphere we can create in our mind and in our life, when it comes to positivity.

Reprogramming your mind toward happiness makes it easier to identify everything that doesn't bring positivity to your life. Your new lens makes happiness the rule, and everything else the exception. It highlights negativity, making you more aware of your surroundings and able to deflect its presence. Make happiness a prerequisite to all things you attempt to do, all people you include in your life, and all the outcomes that you project. Happiness is waiting for you. Let's go get it, starting today.

5

FINDING DAILY HAPPINESS

"Success is the sum of small efforts, repeated day in and day out."

—Robert Collier—

My wife is an amazing cook, and one of her favorite things to make are crêpes. When she goes into the kitchen, she's not looking for pre-made crêpes—she gathers the ingredients: the flour, eggs, butter, vanilla extract, and a few special family secrets in order to make them. Without the right ingredients, there is no crêpe.

Cooking is one of those tasks that reminds us to appreciate the daily effort we put into what we do and how we feel doing it. Cooking requires attention to detail, while enjoying the process, along with exploring individual creativity. With each batch of crêpes my wife prepares, she fine-tunes her recipe, bringing life and love to our bellies and our home.

Life is not about finding quick fixes. Like most things, happiness comes through practice and repetition. Small daily efforts, like gathering ingredients and making a nourishing meal, reinforce positive habit-building, stoke our motivation, and heighten our awareness of all the beauty life has to offer. Small daily efforts create curiosity, excitement, and energy in each moment. Our small daily efforts turn into our habits, building our foundation toward success. Define your cause, your journey, and your future through purposeful daily efforts. Don't just look for success, but search for ways to be successful—one is hopeful for an outcome; the other is proactive in the nature of its journey.

Start small:

Changing your life does not always mean big, radical changes. Small, simple, incremental changes can be just as impactful. For many, the global pandemic was a massive external change, but on an individual level, many of us took the opportunity of our time in quarantine to make small positive changes. Many of my friends started walking outside and getting to know their neighbors like never before. Others began individual self-improvement, nourishing themselves with a new skill. Many of us became more patient, developing an understanding that kindness toward others can go a long way. These small changes have lasting effects, and give focus to how we create energy. New positive habits may take time to build, but never underestimate the power of your daily efforts when your goal is positive change and building positive addictions.

Positive daily addictions:

The word "addiction" has a negative connotation of losing control to something that is bad for you. But, not all addictions are harmful.

I'm addicted to feeling good.

I'm addicted to living out my change.

I'm addicted to the smile I have on my face and the one that I can create for others.

What do these addictions look like in my daily life?

One of my positive daily addictions is eating healthy foods. While many people choose their diet in order to attain a certain shape or look, I choose what I eat based on how it makes me feel. I'm addicted to the way my body functions when I do eat well.

The truth is, we can celebrate being an addict when we're using all of that focus and determination to bring positivity into our lives. Be addicted to making people smile or laugh. Be addicted to loving those around you, constantly finding new ways to share affection and love within your community. Be addicted to being courageous, fighting for what you believe in. Be addicted to living out your desired change on a daily basis.

Be courageous today:

The typical Hollywood blockbuster takes place in a fictional world filled with fabricated truths, layered with plot twists and obstacles, challenging the main character to overcome tremendous adversity. As viewers, we cheer on the main characters, believing they will overcome overwhelming odds just in time to give us our Hollywood ending. We aspire to be as strong as a Marvel superhero, as clever as James Bond, and/or as loving as the lead role in a romantic comedy. More than anything else, we're inspired by the courage these characters exhibit—courage to do what's right, courage to say what needs to be said, courage to help others.

Why do we find it easy to cheer on movie figures for their displays of courage, yet fail to see the courage within ourselves?

If someone was watching a movie about your life, where would they notice displays of courage? I hope it's every day, because, every day you have the opportunity to acknowledge the immense courage you have inside, and be a beacon for others to see their courage through you.

Add time to your day:

Mantras, meditation, yoga, journaling—whatever your morning rituals include, take the time to check in with how you feel and what you want your day to look like.

Live in constant awareness of the moments that each day presents, and use each moment wisely. If you feel anxiety that there simply aren't enough hours, you need to add more time to your day. Reduce your ten-minute shower down to five. Pick your outfit for tomorrow before you go to sleep tonight. Wake up twenty minutes earlier to give yourself the extra time in the morning that usually seems so rushed and programmed. Use the time you lay awake at night before falling asleep to envision the day to come.

Live in authenticity. **The less time you spend trying to be something you're not, the more time you spend being the real version of yourself.** Everyone wishes they could add time to their lives. This is the closest thing to it. Add time to your day, and to your life, by living as many days as you can, in your authentic skin.

Create lists:

Lists help us keep track of what groceries to buy or what to pack for a trip, but there's so much more that lists can help with. Write down lists of creative things that stimulate your mind, lists of things you desire for the future, or lists of your individual skills. Write down lists of all the things you talk about doing or dream of doing. Making a list of your dreams is the first step to seeing them as a reality. The beauty and power of lists is that just seeing things written down on a piece of paper makes them seem more tangible, more realistic, and more likely to happen.

If you don't have a vision, then how will you be able to recognize it, able to capture your dream when it presents itself. Lists recognize the tangible ways of achieving your goals, not letting opportunities slip by without knowing what your're looking for.

Writing something down is a great way to relieve stress, simply by getting it out of your head. Our minds are often crowded, triggering anxiety, thinking we have to have life mapped out within our thoughts. Having lists help clear your mind, creating necessary room for positive thinking.

Silence the ring:

Every time you choose to put your phone on silent, you exercise your personal empowerment. When you put your phone on silent, you are actively choosing to pay attention, to not be distracted, to take time for yourself. If you need to have your phone's ringer on, try this out: each time you hear your phone make a noise, whether it be a text, call, or notification, take a moment before you jump to answer it. You may not have silenced the ring, but you are silencing its interruption within your mind. We don't need to react to each and every sound that comes from our smart devices. Not every text is urgent, and not every notification needs direct attention. We pause our life too often to see what's going on elsewhere, thinking that whatever will be found when we look at our screen will be far more exciting than what we're doing or who we're with. I have seen people stop having fun to answer a non-threatening call. I catch myself telling my daughter to stop doing something she's enjoying, in order for me to try to capture the moment with a photo. By silencing the ring, you show what your priority is: being truly present, in the moment.

Never let people lose to technology. It's ok to lose to a text, a call, with someone on the other side, experiencing connectivity. But let's not lose to an app, a distraction, an update. We're missing opportunities to connect, heal, and learn. Don't miss out on your moments.

Find your "moment":

I have a tough time falling asleep and staying asleep. Once a source of bewilderment and frustration, my lack of sleep has now been turned into my daily source of improvement.

How did I make this switch? I turned frustration into my "moment."

When I'm awake in the middle of the night, I choose not to sit up, staring at the ceiling frustrated, but rather to channel my energy, creating my desired future. I use this time to structure goals or write down quotes of inspiration. It was during one long and restless night in bed that I unknowingly began to write this book. It began as a simple note in my phone, a sentence of inspiration I thought of and wrote down to remember later. I began to feel empowered by turning my authentic thoughts into words and then slowly into sentences and paragraphs. Now, I have a book filled with the product of thousands of these "moments"—moments of creativity despite exhaustion, productivity despite frustration, strength despite weakness.

Excel in your 95%:

Don't miss out on 95% of your life thinking, wishing, or preparing for the pinnacle 5%. Life happens in the 95%.

For many, and especially athletes, this is a difficult thing to accept, but it's what separates the good players from the great players. While good players love to look forward to the games and bright lights, hearing the roar of the crowd, great players know to also enjoy the travel days—days with two practices and the preseason training camps. The journey and the process is the real game preparation.

The 95% presents you with opportunities to improve in specific ways that you can't focus on during the 5%. In the summer, I focus on personal improvement. In preseason, I focus on getting in shape and learning the ins and outs of my team and preparing for the upcoming season. During the season, I focus on team improvement, working on my leadership skills and finding ways to bring who I am to my team. Once I have excelled in my 95%, I am ready for the bright lights of game night.

Whether you're in the 95% or into the 5%, appreciate what you can learn, enjoying each and every moment. This concept applies to high school kids being overly fixated on graduation day instead of their last few months in high school; college kids overly focused on finding an internship to better prepare themselves to get a job after graduation, and so on. Appreciate all of the days leading up to the days—they're all valuable.

Create a new first today:

Having two small children, I'm reminded of the world's beauty by witnessing the excitement in their eyes while experiencing just about everything. The enthusiasm Joy shows for eating a croissant or kicking a ball, helps me not take for granted my 95%. For children, everything is new. As adults, how can we approach our daily life with as much enthusiasm?

Part of why kids are having so much fun is that they are creating and experiencing so many "firsts" in their lives: first day of school, losing a first tooth, first time seeing snow, climbing a tree for the first time. Each day, kids come home with stories of incredible adventure and experiences from their day.

We, as adults, are less likely to encounter things that are completely new to us on a daily basis, but that doesn't mean we can't create firsts for ourselves.

Try a new sexual position in bed for the first time. Be excited about the anticipation of trying it, thinking of it during the day. Take a new route to work for the first time; try a new cereal; wear new clothes for the first time. Go to a new coffee shop that's a minute out of your way or try a new restaurant. Give a friend a new nickname or sleep on the other side of the bed. New surroundings and new interactions stimulate new conversations and new opportunities.

Sounds silly? It's not.

The degree of change is not as important as it is to create and experience more "firsts" in your life. There's an excitement in doing something for the first time, in the anticipation of it, and the event itself. Let's make today a priority to experience at least one first.

Just think about answering friends who ask, "What's new with you?" You can't possibly say, "Same old, same old," when you're trying something new every day. Change the way you live, the way you talk about your day, and the way you feel, by living in constant firsts.

Start a streak today:

Take a ten-minute walk every day. Learn a new word each day. Call someone new each day. Post a positive social update each day. Believe in yourself and know that you are capable and courageous to follow through with the things you start. Each day that you continue your streak will help you build self-confidence through accountability and reliability.

Put happiness on display, today:

Today, your happiness needs to be seen as much as possible, by as many people as possible. Happiness needs to be everywhere you look, reminding you and guiding you throughout the day.

When I was first trying to learn French, I remember putting Post-It notes all around the house so I would walk by them, read the French translations, and learn the words through repetition. These little notes were more than just a vocabulary lesson; they were a constant reminder that learning this language was bringing me joy and creating more opportunities for me to share with my wife and her family.

The world will not stop and send you daily reminders that everything is so great, or remind you to take positive action toward your future. We need to help ourselves with these reminders by putting happiness on display as much as we can. We construct our happiness through the consistency in the choices we make and the repetition in the thoughts we have. Inspire yourself with quotes on the wall, or make a list of things that make you happy and tape it to the refrigerator. Follow inspiring pages on social media, finding people who display their happiness and optimism on a global platform. Put up pictures of places you want to visit. Constantly talk with people, and about things, that promote the positive ideals that make you feel better.

Make it impossible to spend a day without being reminded of the happiness and joy that exists in your life.

Become a daily gambler:

When there is something in your day to win or lose, something on the line, there is an excitement living inside your body. This is not a call to pack your bags and head to Vegas, betting your life's savings on black or red. This is an invitation to be a healthy gambler.

Think of two students challenging each other with a healthy bet on who will score higher on a test. Even the "loser" of the bet will end up scoring a better grade on the test than they would have without the extra challenge and motivation. The idea is not to see who is better or worse but rather to raise the level of daily excitement and increase your curiosity for life, which will increase your physical productivity and your mental creativity; the same way Daven and I challenged each other in college to be the best version of ourselves.

Little bets with friends, coworkers, yourself, and family can spark enthusiasm and bring a special kind of energy to your day. Bet a coworker about who is going to have a more productive week at work. Bet with a friend on who's going to do more for their environment or community this year. Bet with yourself about being able to accomplish something personally that you might not think is possible, keeping track of your process and daily efforts. Even a small bet can create healthy competition and excitement, bringing people closer together and promoting growth; nothing like a little excitement to shake up the day.

Small bets may lead to new challenges, inspiring you to tackle fears and insecurities. Bet a shy friend to sing karaoke in front of a crowd or challenge someone to go skydiving. Bet on who buys an after-work drink and share your stories outside of work, developing a bond with one another. Inspire daily work ethic by having something fun to work for.

What you'll find is that making a daily bet will actually help you hold yourself and other people accountable for the time you all spend during your day. Through bets, you'll spend time helping your community or offering help to others in need. You'll work harder and more efficiently at your job, bringing pride to what you have accomplished through your daily effort. Your success will be measured by the energy you bring and the effect of your inspiration on others. You'll create meaningful relationships and memories by having other people involved and participating in your bets alongside you.

Eliminate frustrations today:

Some frustrations build over time, while others are experienced without any warning. Get to the root of your frustrations, then learn how you can anticipate the next occurrence.

Imagine being a baseball player waiting at the plate for a pitch. Eliminating your frustrations is like having the power to know what pitch is coming next. You may be terrible at hitting a curve ball, but when you know the curve ball is coming, you have a better chance of hitting it. In the same way, you can change the way you approach daily frustrations from a reaction to a preventative action.

Start by identifying what makes you feel frustrated. Turn it into a daily bet with yourself or a friend, or start a new "frustration-free" streak, challenging yourself to not let frustration get the best of you.

I consider myself to be a relatively patient person, but I also like to be active and efficient. It's easy to premeditate frustration if I feel that things are moving too slowly or will be done inefficiently. When I spend time with my large family, I realize that there are a lot of transitional moments and times I find myself waiting around for people to get ready—moments that could be filled with frustration. My wife's family starts dinner around 6:00 p.m., and I might not eat until midnight. Instead of waiting for things to happen, or for people to be ready to do something, or to eat, I turn my focus and energy elsewhere. If I have fifteen to thirty minutes, I write, watch a show, text or call a friend, do the dishes, work out, or meditate. I anticipate this frustration by having things ready to do if I am presented with extra time. An added benefit is that, by pre-occupying myself, I alleviate the stress and pressure I put on other people, not making them feel rushed by my impatience. Identify your frustrations so that you can proactively turn it into action, anticipation into productivity.

Look for light in tough moment today:

Some days, there are no words or actions to alleviate the pain we feel. Some days, we have to accept the darkness as being dark. Feelings are meant to be felt, no matter where they fall on the spectrum. If you experience a tough moment today, don't give into the darkness, but search for the light. If you accept darkness as a possibility in life, then you must also believe that light can be an alternative. If you're willing to look, knowing both options exist, you will see there is always light, no matter how dark it seems.

Sadness will come. Sadness has arrived. I can get through it. I will find the light.

Fight fears today:

Fear exists in the looking, not the leaping. When I was twelve, I went on a field trip with my class to an outdoor ropes course. At the end of the course, there was a "trust jump," where each kid would jump off a twenty-foot ledge and grab hold of a bar dangling out in front of them. I remember watching my classmates stand on the ledge—their bodies frozen—while they contemplated whether they could, or couldn't, make the jump.

Then . . . they jumped.

Adrenalin and excitement took over, as they realized that it didn't matter if they caught the bar or not—everyone safely repelled down to the ground. Once they got down and looked back up, they gained perspective and felt proud of what they had accomplished. We all then joked with one another, agreeing that it seemed so much higher when we were up there looking down.

When I was thirty, I went to a similar place and attempted the same jump. As an adult attempting the same feat, I realized that the scariest part was just standing on the platform looking at the bar.

So why does fear hold a prominent place in our minds?

People often ask me if I am scared or nervous when taking game-winning shots and playing in big moments. They wonder how I handle playing in front of large crowds, with so much on the line. The truth is, I only notice the crowd when the clock is stopped. Otherwise, I'm too focused on playing the game itself. Just play; just do. Fear may be there, but I only notice it when I'm not in motion.

When you leap, fear fades.

Take the trash out today:

When we receive junk mail, we simply delete it. It is time to unsubscribe.

There are a lot of different types of junk that come our way each and every day.

Life can be filled with spam, creating a speed bump to personal development and discovering happiness. Unsubscribe to anything that might be hindering your growth and future success. Unsubscribe from all the naysayers and all the nonbelievers. Take the time to find out who and what information is holding you back, and learn how to avoid its influence all together. There is a big difference between continually having to delete all the negative influence in your life versus taking time to unsubscribe once and for all. Your effort and focus should be on creating a positive future, not continually spending energy deleting negative and useless distractions.

Your daily chart toward happiness:

Take a look at these common stressors:

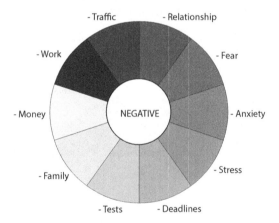

If you were to create your own chart, what are the ten things you'd include that bring you constant stress or fear? Could you identify which stress occupies most of your time, based on how much it consumes your mind or how often you stress about it?

Now, make a new table; only this time, just include ten things that bring you happiness and joy—the things you're thankful for on a daily basis.

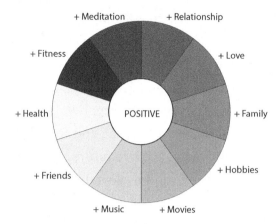

Lastly, make a table that includes both your stressors and the things that bring you happiness and positivity. You only have space for ten things total—the ten that occupy the most time in your day.

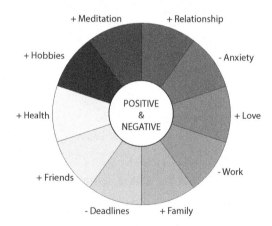

Do any of your stressors make it into the final chart? Do the positive things in your life consume enough space and time in your mind, and in your thoughts to outweigh the stressors?

Each day, work to shave off percentages of your stressors—no matter how big or small—and replace it with a new positive label, or enhance what's already positive in there.

Stress won't ever go away completely, but what can change is the way we allow ourselves small moments to stress out and feel anxious. For professional basketball players, stress normally revolves around game-time performances. Okay, allow yourself to stress a little before the game, during warm-ups or pregame speeches. The trick is to release the stress from the other areas of your day and other areas of your life, letting anxiety only have the smallest amount of energy possible.

Take a look back at the stressors you wrote down in your table and imagine what these stressors will mean to you in twenty years. Do you think that you will even remember today's stress in 20 years?

If they won't matter in twenty years, why give them so much influence today?

Define yourself today:

I often tell my mom, "That was yesterday; let it go."

We both laugh because it's not quite that easy, but the reality is that yesterday doesn't need to define today in any way, shape, or form. Today, you recreate who you are, being confident in the new-and-improved you that only exists today.

I get excited about new things, new ideas, and expressing new thoughts. I challenge the person I see in the mirror with ideas of the new person I can become, starting today. I remind myself that yesterday was the old me and that I have the capability to be who I want to be today—I have the choice.

I recently watched *Game Changers*, a documentary about high-level athletes who eat a plant-based diet. After watching the film, I decided to change my diet and lifestyle. I became a new me, with a new commitment to my health and well-being. I love the new me—confident in my choice but also fully aware that, in the future, I may learn new information that compels me to redefine myself again. Or, I may simply miss the taste of In-N-Out Burger too much and break my diet. I will always remain open to new information and positive influences that may be coming my way, looking for new ways to add to my positive addictions. Every day, there are new breakthroughs and new information that help us evolve in the way we think and the way we live, which is one of the best parts about being alive today. We can't box ourselves into old habits and old routines, thinking it's impossible to recreate who we are or be inspired by new stimulus.

Too often, we feel the restraints of the boxes we place around ourselves and those that others place around us, as well. We feel that we must be who we are expected to be, who the world wants us to be, or what version of ourselves that makes us feel the safest. Break through the box, becoming the person you are meant to be, not the one who you're supposed to be.

It's not a weakness to change; it's a weakness to be closed-minded to new ideas and growth. I am excited and confident in who I am today, and I'm not afraid to change and evolve tomorrow.

Enjoy a Saturday morning today:

Single friends often ask me, "What should I look for in a potential partner?" My response has always been the same: it's not about who you're with on Friday night; it's about who you want to be with on Saturday morning.

Many of us find the courage to be the person we want when the lights are on, when the party is going, and when the world is rotating in our favor. It's the aftermath of these moments that define the character and foundation of who we are. Saturday mornings lead to the self-confidence and motivation we have as individuals to live out the rest of our week to its full potential. They are the quiet mornings in which we see the truest reflection in the mirror, and we look back with loving admiration. Your new vision, and new positive foundation, create a Saturday morning that is just as exciting and impactful as a Friday night. So, enjoy who you see in the mirror, enjoy your Saturday—every day.

Eliminate excuses today:

Are you making excuses for not taking the opportunities and chances you are offered?

Making excuses almost guarantees that you won't reach your full potential or compete at your highest level. Excuses manifest in your mind and slowly turn into a reason—a reason for not improving, not inspiring, and not achieving. A reason for not ultimately being happy. Excuses have the ability to take on a life of their own and define who we are. An excuse can turn into your story.

But when you eliminate the excuse, then you eliminate the hurdle. So, don't let the hurdles turn into a wall; instead, clear the way, in order for you to see your day in a new light.

Today's constant perspective:

When you feel healthy, remember what it feels like to be sick. When you are working out and running, remember what it's like to be in pain on the sidelines. When you shower, remember to be thankful for fresh water. When you sit in the sun, remember the days you're inside while it's raining. When you go back to work, sit in traffic, and deal with deadlines, still remember to be thankful for your job, able to leave confinement.

Be happy for the things you know and happy to have a mind capable of learning the things you don't. Happy for the things you have and happy for the ability to work for the things you don't. Fortunes and misfortunes, wins and losses—your journey is your blessing. So, be thankful for it all.

Change your "I have to's" into "I get to's" today:

With each new opportunity comes a choice: you either "have to" do it or you "get to" do it. There is significant power in the elimination of "I have to's" in your daily approach. A simple change in words can lead to a freedom and excitement that is infectious—one that can help your mind appreciate all the things you're lucky enough to be a part of. When you "get to" do something, you are elated with the opportunity, rather than being forced to deal with it.

Today is special:

Imagine the feeling you have before a first date, a birthday weekend, a bachelor party, or hosting friends and family for holidays. These special times bring out the best in us. During these special times, we make the extra effort to give the best that we have to offer, focusing on people, giving the benefit of the doubt, and showing increased kindness. In special moments, we become more excited, more patient, and a better version of ourselves with the people we love. This is how we live out our Christmas Theory.

I have had the pleasure of hosting many of my friends from other states and countries in my home in Santa Barbara. My wife and I get excited to see the people we love as we prepare the house for their arrival; a nice clean home, a special home-cooked meal, and, most importantly, our attention and energy.

When we are faced with a "normal" day—seemingly nothing special to look forward to—we still have the potential within us to be at our best. Every day, we have the ability to show the people we're with that they are special to us. We create the energy that circulates around us by our approach and the way we feel about the things we get to experience in life. By treating today, and every day, as special, we have the ability to effect change through our appreciation and love.

Improve a hat today:

We all walk around with many titles, many things that come together and create the person we are. We are parents and children. Sisters and brothers. Friends and coworkers. Recognize the many hats you wear and make today special by improving on at least one of them, doing something special in that area. Today, I was an amazing dad or an amazing son, which makes today a good day.

Create love in the transitions:

When we transition from one thing to another, we leave a lasting impression in that space and create an impression on the next space that we enter. If we leave a warm and loving house, then we are more excited to return home after work, optimistically feeling love will be waiting for us when we return. The way we say hello and goodbye, the way we hug and greet one another, the way we smile at one another, talk to one another, and listen to one another—all of these small transitions make up the lasting feeling we have for the day, and for the people we interact with.

Think about the way you want to be received in whatever environment you are coming into. What kind of person do you want waiting for you when you open the door? What kind of person will you be when you're the one waiting for someone else? Transitional love creates that undefinable feeling of contentment and happiness in the world you live in.

Live in the journey today:

Relationships provide meaning to our life and heavily influence our journey. Healthy relationships mean that we are never someone's solution, just a positive piece to their individual puzzle. We must seek out our own journey individually, using our own lens to find our authenticity. Find your path today by realizing where to look and being confident in who's doing the looking. The most powerful thing to know about reading this book, its true purpose, is not to have you replicate my journey, but to use my message to enhance your own journey.

Seek out new pieces to life's puzzle:

There is something to learn from everyone you meet and every situation you encounter. I have encountered different people and experienced different cultures and ideologies. I like to believe that, as a father, I will incorporate pieces from the diverse life that I have lived, using all positive aspects to enhance the lives of my children. I search for new additions to my life, new pieces, in order to create a well-rounded experience and an open mind for my family.

In every person and every experience, there are new pieces to the puzzle of life:

Learn creativity from a young entrepreneur.
Learn dedication and hard work from an athlete or your favorite teacher.
Learn love and compassion from a mother or father, grandmother or grandfather.
Learn about other cultures from people around the world.
Learn expression and attention to detail from an artist.
Look for pieces all around us that can enhance our minds and our evolutionary process of growth.

The people around you are filled with unique pieces that can help you grow. You don't need to travel to be worldly; you just need to have an eager and open mind toward what's out there.

Turn "sorry" into action today:

*"All I do is say sorry; half the time, I don't even know what
I'm saying it about."*

—Mac Miller—

The word "sorry" can be overused, underused, and dangerous to self-improvement. But, "sorry" can be turned into something productive when words turn to action.

The importance of being sorry is not found in the word itself but rather in the action that follows. Turning sorry into an action means focusing on the future instead of the past. Cut out any anxiety over yesterday by giving yourself a chance to change it today. Own up to your mistakes, having confidence in the person you are and your character moving forward. Sorry is no longer about feeling ashamed or useless, sorry can inspire action toward improvement.

Create your future today:

What future are you fighting for? And when are you fighting for it?

Each summer, I am faced with tough decisions when choosing the right path for my family and my career before signing a new contract. I am trying to find the right contract for the present, while putting myself in the best position to also create the right career for my future.

New contracts determine which team I will be playing for, in which country, and for how long. I spend lots of time on the phone with my agent going through all the pros and cons of each offer we receive. Often, we discuss the idea that this year's contract has the potential to set up a great opportunity for next year. It's important to both of us to have a vision and a plan for my future career, as well as what's best for now.

Many decisions are made while looking into the future, creating a hypothetical idea of what's to come and what life might look like. But what happens if I keep making decisions based on future years to come?

The future is never promised to anyone, especially an athlete. Covid-19 ended my season in Greece and changed the world for millions of people. We all had a vision for what the year would hold for us, and life had its own way of altering that vision.

The future is uncertain, but we get to actively create our future with our daily decisions. Today creates tomorrow.

Find what you are looking for today:

2020 exposed many cracks and tears in the fabric of our society and how we take care of one another, and it is more than justified to feel upset, victimized, and alone.

Remember this: whatever you look for, it's there—you'll find it.

Need sympathy? Look in any direction, and you can find a sympathetic ear to justify your unhappiness and agree that the adversity you're experiencing may be just too much to overcome. Go searching, and you'll find unrest, injustice, divisiveness, and sadness all around, as well as people to match.

Or, in your heart of hearts, are you looking for more for yourself and for others? Scary thing is, only you can ask, and honestly answer this questions for yourself.

If you look hard enough in the other direction, you'll find motivation and strength. You'll find unity and inspiration. You can find happiness and optimism, as well as people who are looking for the same thing. Be sure that, whatever it is that you're actively seeking, you will find it. Today begins a search for the reality you want to create for tomorrow.

Take one step today:

I never thought I would write a book, and if someone would have asked me to write one, I would have had no idea where to begin, overwhelmed by its enormity. This book wasn't written in a day, or even a year. It was one step, taken each day, that compounded my effort into something I could never have imagined.

Today can be the start of your book—the beginning of your development into something more. Sometimes, even taking a step back is leading you in the right direction. Every sentence I deleted or edited out of this book was one step closer to where I wanted the book to be. Your imprint on this world—your legacy—is created with each step you take—forward, backward, sideways, and so on. Your effort will never go unnoticed, especially when you value it yourself.

Write a book, paint a picture, learn a dance, share meaningful conversations, or speak out for justice, spreading love to people around you in all that you do. Your authenticity is visible through your contribution. Your existence is worthy of a story and documentation. Begin to create your individual imprint one step at a time.

Make adjustments today:

As an athlete, I can appreciate and admire the mental focus and concentration of great golfers. The golf swing, in short, consists of a backwards motion adding momentum to a forward swing as the golfer strikes the ball. Each tiny adjustment of the swing affects the trajectory, and each golfer has their own unique swing. The difference between good and great golfers is their repetition and their ability to adjust their swing midway through the stroke. Great golfers even have the ability to stop when they feel like something is off, and then regroup before hitting their shot.

Having awareness of your position and being able to control your trajectory by making adjustments is the key to a great golf shot and is also key to navigating your journey through life. Be aware today of the direction, or motion, your life is taking. When things are going well, be thankful for your movement, swinging with confidence. When you notice any discomfort or deviation, have the awareness to stop and take control of the situation. Pause for a second, setting yourself back on the course that you desire.

Even when you think life is moving in the wrong direction, your in-the-moment adjustments can have a positive effect on your forward progress. In golf, to hit the ball forward, you must first use the momentum of a backswing. The golf swing teaches us that going backwards is just as important to reaching our goals as when we are moving forward. When I watch a golf swing, I don't think that each person is swinging backwards, away from their goal. I know that going backwards will build momentum for stronger forward movement. 2020 may have felt like a setback, like we've made zero progress, when, in fact, it very well may be setting us up for something even stronger in the future.

Add a percent today:

Happiness is not experienced in absolutes—you are not living in 100% happiness or sadness all the time. Part of the excitement of each day is finding new ways to improve in order to make today better than yesterday.

What can you do to increase your happiness by 1%?

Even when life is challenging us through adversity, we can be focused on achieving that 1%, giving purpose to our day, and focusing on the daily improvement and excitement of building a better tomorrow.

Smile today:

"Let us always meet each other with a smile, for the smile is the beginning of love."

—Mother Teresa—

Sometimes, all you need in life is the benefit of the doubt.

Change your world with a smile. A smile encourages people to meet you and listen to you, feeling comforted with your energy. A smile can often be a first impression that you make on someone, or a lasting effect on someone's perception of who you are. A first encounter is very influential, as initial perceptions are hard to change.

Create the benefit of the doubt for yourself by being a constant smiler. When your down days come, and you're not performing at your highest level, you will be met with understanding from a friend or from a boss. People will respond differently, thinking, "I wonder if he is okay . . . He's usually smiling—something might be off."

We begin to live out our change with a smile, giving people the right perception of who we want them to see.

Change how you are perceived today:

How many people really take the time to get to know you for the person you truly are? Even after a smile, often, we are misjudged—defined by someone else's perception of who we are and what we're all about. How we're perceived is a high-stakes situation, one that can have a lasting impact on your success in relationships, in love, and in life.

Do people perceive you as standoffish, moody, irritable, impatient, or seemingly aggressive or unfriendly? If you are perceived this way at work, when you underperform, bosses and coworkers will rarely give you a second chance to perform or provide a platform for explanation. People will be less likely to extend invitations of help, warmer daily interactions will be sparse, and people will rarely invest their time to get to know you as a person. When you're perceived in a negative way, others may believe, "That's just the way she is, and I don't want anything to do with her."

When you are perceived as a happy, loving, fun, friendly person, the world becomes a little more understanding and accommodating. Co-workers may come to you for help and open themselves up as an ally or someone they can count on for help. Inclusion comes your way in the office and out, as you may seem like a fun person to be around.

What a monumental difference . . . Perception influences the way people treat you and the way they communicate with you. While you might be the same person with the same performance, if you're perceived negatively or positively, you're not treated the same.

When we smile, we change the way the world perceives us. A smile can lead to a friendship, giving people the chance, and the desire, to get to know you. A smile can be the trigger—the butterfly effect—that changes how you're perceived, sparking a change in your entire day, and maybe your entire life.

Be thankful for support today:

I remind myself daily to think of all the people who have played a role in me becoming the person I am today. From my grandparents to my children, and everyone in between. Countless individuals have raised and supported me since I was a baby. We all have a supporting cast, which has played a role in molding the person we see in the mirror.

How are you showing your thankfulness for all these individuals?

We can show thankfulness through our daily attitude and the effort we give, by living out the change we desire, and being our truest self. We must give our time—life's most valued possession—to finding our passions, seeking out the best life has to offer.

For those who feel unsupported in your daily life, you have the opportunity to change the tide. Today is your day to seek out people who bring energy and light. Today is also the day to realize that you have the potential to be the support system that other people may be lacking. Understand your desire for help, your desire to feel wanted, and know that people around you share that same feeling. We are all looking for connectivity, and today can be the day that you reach out and show your support.

Discover a new mantra today:

Mantras are your quick guide to realignment and focus. Mantras help establish positive habits, creating banks for the river, not allowing you to get off course during your day. Mantras are personal and speak to your individual goals and dreams. Here are a few of mine:

Today is a gift; treat today as if it is an audition for tomorrow, because it is.

I am living the change I want to see in the world.

I can always learn from others to improve myself.

Turn away from screens and turn toward people.

Say what you "can" do, and do what you say.

Be thankful for all things.

Don't highlight problems; be the solution.

I am the author of my own story.

Success starts today.

Live in endless thankfulness.

I am active in my own happiness.

Success should never come as a surprise. The work you put in each day grows with interest, like adding money to your bank account. The progress you make each day—in public and in private—is paving the way for your success.

When the day is over, be confident in being able to say that you have improved your life. You have developed a new skill. You have encouraged growth in someone else. You have improved the way you see the world or the way the world perceives you. Your success is coming, and your effort, each day, is at the core of making it a reality.

Start your best year today:

Will 2020 be remembered throughout history as being the year that changed the world . . . for the better? Don't wait for adversities to pass, thinking that the person you desire to be is just waiting on the other side of a pandemic or whatever hardship you're currently facing.

While some may think, "Why us?," "Why now?" and become upset with what we're experiencing, others are thankful for such a unique time to realign their journey. We have been offered a moment in which the whole world is living through collective change, wanting to be inspired, feel excited, and positively grow. When do we start? How do we start?

Buy a calendar today and hang it on the wall. Open the calendar to this month and find your day. Take a pen and write in bold letters: "Today is my day for change."

Look at the calendar each day, reminding yourself that your day for change is coming. This change doesn't depend on anyone or anything but yourself. Envision the changes you desire, for yourself and for the world, detailing how that will play out in your daily life. Give this change the proper details and mental design that is needed to be ready for the day to arrive. Don't limit yourself with doubt or

Sunday	Monday	Tuesday	Wednesday	Thursday	Friday	Saturday
1	2	3	4	5	6	7
8	9	10	11	12	13	14
15	16	17	18	19	20	21
22	23	24	25	26	27	28
29	30	31				

Today is my day for change!

confine yourself to any type of enclosure, daring to dream bigger and bigger each day. Create the life you desire one day at a time. Inspire yourself to be reinvented and to constantly improve. Don't wait for a wedding, a birth announcement, or a funeral to have these conversations with yourself. Use constant perspective to make every day meaningful.

Life is happening, and we are the lucky ones able to experience it. We get to change the world—one day at a time.

6

YOUR HAPPIEST YOU

"I thought the NBA could be a big option, but the journey is different for everybody. If I look back, I have no regrets. I came to Europe, I played in the EuroLeague, I experienced many different things, I won many titles, played with great teammates and for great coaches, for some of the most historical teams in Europe. The NBA has always been a dream, but today, I'm kind of glad that dream didn't come true. I realized that my real dream was another and it was to compete to win titles here in Europe."

—Kyle Hines—

Professional basketball player and four-time EuroLeague champion

I often think of my ten-year-old self, wondering if he would agree with the decisions I've made, the person I have become, and the mindset I now have.

The hardest professional basketball decision I ever made was in the summer of 2015, after coming off of an amazing season in Russia. With individual and team success came many offers from high-level clubs, as my hard work opened many new and exciting doors.

When the season ended, I went to France with Agathe to spend time with family to unwind. I remember receiving a phone call from my agent while we were driving from Le Mans to Paris. "A couple of NBA teams want to see you for an individual workout," he told me. To me, the NBA is the top league in the world—the pinnacle of basketball success. This was it. The dream, right?

Agathe and I talked for hours about what it would mean to go back to the United States and do the workouts, potentially play in the NBA, or stay and sign with one of the European clubs. We evaluated what it meant for me to be successful, and for our family to be happy. Through deep soul communication, one intense dream, and conversations with Agathe, I was able to hone in on my true goals and what aspects of my career brought me the most happiness. I chose to sign a deal to come back and play in Europe with one of the top clubs. Why?

My goal was to feel alive in the process. My success was in the journey, in the day-to-day, and in making the most of my 4th quarters. My happiest self is one that is driven with my own set of rules and my own path toward happiness. I realized, more than ever, that I was already living my dream.

Each decision that I have made has helped shape the person I am, influencing my journey toward happiness. I don't have any doubt about my success, knowing that I am my best self when I am honest and true about what brings me happiness, authenticity, and joy.

My success is defined by the love I feel when I play the game and the inspiration I bring to others. My success is felt by the size of my smile when I arrive at practice, when I'm on the court, and when I leave each game, no matter the result. I believe wholeheartedly in my ability, feeling that I can be an all-star in any league—NBA included. Who knows if I would have gotten the job, loved the NBA, or just had a workout? There are many things I don't know. But I know I'm happy, and that I love the choices I have made.

I will always choose optimism, ready to take on any challenge. My time in both Europe and China provided a stage for me to inspire the world through playing the game I love, the way I wanted to play it. In almost every game I have competed in, I was on the court, and my teammates looked to me to have the ball in my hands in those game-defining moments. I am happiest when I play a key role in the game-winning decisions. I am happiest when I am creating happiness for others, able to inspire through my leadership on and off the court.

Soon after the birth of our daughter, my wife asked me if my perspective on life had changed. Since becoming a father, I have felt a new daily purpose, desiring to share the lessons I've learned and the qualities I've acquired with the next generation. I imagine myself being the first runner in the most important relay race, in which I must pass the baton to the next generation, offering them a better world than I had. The positives I am able to pass down will be my measure of success, as my children will be equipped with a newly inspired heart for equality, love, and happiness for all.

This hope for my children comes with a huge responsibility—I must constantly have these qualities, these strengths, on display. If kids are truly like sponges, then what are they going to absorb when they see my actions and hear my words? If our children do deserve the best, then we must give them our best. Our responsibility is not just to try our best for ourselves, but rather to realize that our happiness is not just for us; it's for the whole world.

Finding your happiness may be met with doubt and/or disbelief from the outside world, as it is natural to challenge different ideals and unfamiliar territory. Know that your path is not the same as anyone else's, feeling confident in your journey—authentic in each step. Happiness can come through privilege or misfortune, as 2020 was a combination of both. It can be transferred from person to person, or grow organically from within.

Happiness is found in the freedom of thought and the expression of our passions. It is heard in the sound of our song, as we bring beauty to life all around us. It is free from all restraints, all boxes, and all pressures. It is unique and tailor-made for each of us individually.

> "All inventive and creative people, they're not hung up on fixed definitions of what any form of life or reality may be."
>
> **—Wayne Gretzky—**

It's up to us to create our own definition of happiness. We get to design the blueprint for our success and for what our best selves look like. There is no fixed definition, no one with the power to tell you that you don't deserve happiness in all its forms. You have the freedom to live out your dream.

In our process to find happiness for ourselves and others, we must remain thankful—thankful through it all.

Be thankful in good times, giving thanks to the ones who got you there. Be thankful in adverse times by giving thanks to the people who you can rely on.

Be thankful in times of complacency by giving thanks for the opportunities life has to offer.

Be thankful just because you are who you are.

When your happiness has a foundation of thankfulness, you realize that each moment has purpose, power, and meaning.

Happiness is not authentic if you're walking on egg shells, unable to use your true voice, or confined by external boxes. To be you, you must be authentically you. Walking on egg shells requires you to suppress your true self, in order to promote a sense of security for others around you. Remain you, knowing that authenticity is a risk—a risk worth taking.

Finding happiness in your scouting report:

"That's why I tell people we focus too much on stats and not story. Stats are like, 'What college are you from?' But your story is like, 'What was your grandfather like? Who was your favorite relative and why?' I think what makes you more than a stat is, once you see yourself, you see yourself as more than a stat, and you start thinking about, 'Who are you? What do you care about? What brings you joy?'"

—Michelle Obama—

In basketball, there are papers called scouting reports that are given to players before a game, containing descriptions of each player on the opposing team. Scouting reports also contain statistical analysis, recording contributions on the court, like shooting percentages and how many rebounds each player averages.

I read these scouting reports to understand my opponents, as well as the individual tendencies of each player. Scouting reports critique what players can do and what they can't do, highlighting strengths and weaknesses. Over the years, I have made a lot of friends who play for teams I compete against. I often ask them to let me see the scouting report of my team, including the pages about me.

My scouting report hasn't changed all that much since the day I became a pro. My strengths and weaknesses haven't deviated dramatically. Reading my own scouting report is humbling. Your weaknesses and strengths are there for all to see. While some may be discouraged by the things they can't do, others are encouraged with the things they can.

When reading these reports it's important to keep the perspective that, no matter what you do, there will always be weaknesses on your scouting report. You can perceive this to mean that you'll never be good enough, or you can find relief, knowing that there is always a better you to reach for, but never a perfect you. I have spent so much of my life dedicated to my craft, and no matter how hard I work, there are certain things I lack and certain weaknesses that I possess. There are games where I play well, and some where I play poorly. Each day is a chance to learn and improve, as I'm focused on my contribution and not on achieving perfection, like the boy I worked with in China. My effort is what's constant.

Scouting reports have taught me a great lesson about happiness, as you can ask any high-level player, and they will tell you that these stats do not reflect the whole story. It's impossible to measure character and contribution with numbers and analytics. The effect you have on the people around you can't be calculated by a number or statistic; it is felt in your presence and overall contribution to whatever it is you're a part of. Your measure of happiness is defined by you, and those who you inspire—not by stats on a page.

So what would your scouting report say?

It's not so easy to see yourself in this light—exposing limitations—especially when it's written down on a piece of paper.

This is not meant to focus on weakness, but rather a realization of strength and empowerment. It's in my own weakness where I find my strength. When you know who you are, you're able to look in the mirror and identify what you're good at and what you want to work on. I accept my weaknesses, looking for ways to learn from other teammates or coaches. I accept my strengths and try to pick teams or leagues that will use me for what I can provide, to improve the team. I cover the weaknesses of my other teammates anyway I can by utilizing my strengths. I turn to my teammates to pick up my slack, where I am less productive, as we work to become a good team through our relationships and understanding of one another.

Surround yourself with people who know you and are, able to make you stronger. Build a community around yourself with the highest probability for success. Find people to believe in, and those who believe in you. Find strength in your humility and true understanding of yourself.

I have had the unique pleasure of growing up with a very close core group of friends in Santa Barbara. Now, for over half my life, I have been away from home, following my dream wherever the basketball road has taken me. My boys, each uniquely different, have supported me and my life, no matter what. We are loving and accepting of one another, supportive of the individual path each one of us has chosen. We bring out the best in one another, instead of being envious or comparing ourselves through competition.

I remember the first time Agathe came to America and met my friends. She was surprised by the diversity of our group, remarking on the significantly different ways in which we live our lives. I learned that this was rare and lucky, as we have always felt comfortable with one another, where we can be ourselves, and have always felt accepted as such. My friends have helped shape me into my truest and happiest self. Acceptance from yourself, and from the closest ones around you, allow your happiest self to thrive through a foundation of security and trust.

My best self is a "work in progress."

My current situation doesn't define me or my story. My kindness surpasses my circumstance. My effort reflects my heart, not my job description or duty. I seek out purpose, realizing the power of being active in my happiness.

Happiness in stages:

Not every stage in my career brought me over-the-top happiness, but I stayed the course, thankful for the strength each day to fight for new goals. Everything from injuries to changing schools, to changing teams, has impacted my happiness in some way or another. Even today, I am constantly traveling and working in different countries.

While exciting, this lifestyle comes with significant uncertainty, especially for my family, who supports me.

Within each stage, you can identify personal joy or feel uncomfortable waiting for something better. Count your blessings before your frustrations. Starting with the positive gives your mind the right headspace to deal with the latter.

Happiness is in the little things:

Happiness is all around us, even if it's not captured on a phone or recorded for others to witness. Your happiest self isn't just found in your weekly posts and updates, but rather in the small moments of your day.

Would you buy the happiness you're selling?

It's not enough to want others to think that you're happy; you need to feel happiness and believe it from the inside out.

Imagine being a salesperson, and what you're trying to sell is your own happiness. The best salesperson is one that truly believes in the product.

After finishing my collegiate career, I went to a couple of NBA pre-draft workouts. Some teams assessed more than just my basketball skills, requiring a written section and an interview process. I remember some of the questions I was asked about my mentality as a basketball player. They asked if I envisioned myself failing, or if I had anxiety of not performing well. I didn't think much of the questions at the time, thinking that they were just assessing my level of confidence.

As I learn more about the state of mind of so many athletes and the mental instability they face, I now understand the significance of the questions. To believe in yourself is to understand the power that happiness has on impacting your success, not the other way around. Even though it wasn't what he initially envisioned, Kyle Hines found his recipe for happiness, and it came through an authentic understanding of who he is and the substance of his journey. He chose happiness, and it became the recipe for his success.

Your journey may deviate, challenging you and surprising you at every turn. Know that there are so many paths to find happiness inside you, more than you could have ever imagined.

INSPIRE INSPIRATION

Does the power of tomorrow provide enough motivation for you to create a better world today?

To inspire is to believe in something greater than yourself. We have the opportunity now to inspire a future that is exciting and worth looking forward to, worth fighting for, and worth sharing with everyone. We can be the inspiration by designing a future that we believe in.

2020 can be a symbolic start—the chance to actualize our dreams with A New 20/20 Vision.

It's time to go back to work . . . What kind of job are you looking for?
It's time to reprogram adversity . . . What attitude will you bring to your life?
It's time to interact with family . . . What kind of love are you sharing?
It's time to listen and learn from one another . . . What kind of compassion do you have?
It's time to date and look for love . . . What will you be looking for?
It's time to inspire . . . What is your message?

Inspiration is knowing who you are and sharing your story to the world. Generational happiness can be passed down from parent to child or transferred from friend to friend, becoming a mindset for the future to adopt.

Halfway through one season in Greece, my wife and I shared a conversation about how we felt the season was going. I was trying to be my optimistic self, telling her that everything was good and that I felt great about my team and my role as a player.

Agathe told me that she wanted more for me. She told me that she wanted me to play for a different team because my role on this team wasn't the same as before, and that I seemed less inspiring as a player.

Putting my ego aside helped me realize that she was right. My lack of creativity and inspired play led to a watered-down version of my skills and attitude. I don't need to score 100 points in every game to be inspiring, but the crowd needs to feel my heart by the way I play. She went on to say that, no matter the score, when I am playing like myself, and acting like myself, my passion is seen by whomever is watching.

This led to some incredible soul communication as I reflected on the season and my entire career. When people ask me about my career, I want to inspire them by talking about the people I've met along the way and the places I was fortunate enough to live in. I want to share stories about the countries I've visited and the knowledge I have gained. I want my answer to be much more than about the points I scored, the assists I made, or the games I won. I want to tell stories about the people who inspired me along my journey and stories of the things I have done to inspire others.

I will inspire people by telling them about the power of connectivity and that we are all beautiful exactly the way we are. I will inspire others not by telling them they don't understand me, but by opening up my heart so they can.

I will inspire others by reminding them of these truths:

It doesn't take doing something big to be someone big.

It doesn't take moving the world to reshape its construct for yourself or someone else.

It doesn't take winning the game to inspire the crowd.

It doesn't take a formal education to be educated.

The world is a beautiful place, and we have the ability to make it even better.

Growing up in Santa Barbara, CA, one of my favorite places to have lunch was a place called Village Cheese and Wine (or Wine and Cheese to locals). For myself, and thousands of others, going to get a sandwich at Wine and Cheese meant you were going to see John. Locals and visitors alike can share at least one great story about its late owner, John. Was John ever popular on TV or in a movie? No, I don't think so. Did he have millions of dollars in the bank? Probably not . . . Was he admired as a celebrity, positively affecting and inspiring everyone he encountered? Absolutely. While John may no longer be with us, he continues to inspire us.

I believe that people are more inspired by the story behind a person than the people themselves. Inspiration comes less from people inheriting millions of dollars and more from the story of someone making their way to the top from having less, carving a new path, inventing something new, inspiring new thoughts, and giving back

John

their effort for the benefit of others. Stories about overcoming adversity, taking risks, and experiencing the road less traveled, brings courage to many. People don't show up to acceptance speeches to marvel at the award itself, but rather to be inspired by the story of the individual and the journey that got them to the podium.

Organic inspiration:

To truly inspire, you must focus on sharing your organic abilities with the world. Everyone has God-given abilities—special talents of athleticism, musicality, or humor. God-given abilities may bring admiration, or even fame, but they won't inspire on their own. It is **you** that people want to know—**you** that will inspire them.

Inspire others by spending time with them and sharing your message, leaving them with a new outlook, encouraging them to seek more for themselves.

Every moment of weakness is an opportunity to inspire strength. You can inspire through your highest peaks and your lowest valleys, in times of transition, and times of adversity.

You are the product of everything good in your life added with every tough moment. You can use everything you have learned and all your experiences to become the best version of yourself, ready to inspire the world.

Inspiration is understanding your mortality and breathing life into everything that you can, while you can. Inspiration comes from knowing that you have a story to tell and the courage to tell it; it is found within your fight to overcome all challenges, and sharing gratitude and thankfulness for everything along the way.

Finding what inspires you:

You can draw inspiration from all walks of life. Speak with the youth, keeping your mind fresh through new ideas and understanding what's relevant now and what's to come. Youth have uninhibited optimistic ideas for an unknown future, reminding us that life is something to be excited about, not something to fear.

Speak with your elders, who can help guide you toward success if you're willing to listen and learn from their stories, from their pain and happiness. Elders have a way of reminding you that there is no better time than now to accomplish whatever it is you desire. A calming voice, reminding us to slow down, to realize who we are and what brings us happiness—a much needed reminder that we can release much of the anxiety and stress we feel on a daily basis.

Speak with people from all around the world to uncover alternative truths. You will have a much better understanding of your authenticity, when you have learned what authenticity looks like in others. Use this knowledge to inspire, through purposeful words filled with a new voice of hope for our future.

> "Inspiration is the metric that dictates whether or not a project is a success . . . if you tell me the goal is to inspire. That makes our job a lot easier."
>
> **—Nipsy—**

When our goal is to inspire, we can accomplish it in all that we do, through our effort and our kind heart toward positive change. We inspire by being a reflection of happiness—a pair of glasses through which people can use to view the world through new lenses. I find my happiest self in knowing that my purpose is empowered by the message I am giving to the world and inspiring change for the future. I use inspiration as my driving force. I believe my message has value, and I'm rich in knowing my capability to motivate and inspire.

To inspire is to understand. The best speeches, and the best speakers, have the ability to recognize their audience and reach them on a deep personal level. This is achieved through knowledge of the audience and finding a common ground of love and respect for one another. Learn to bend your message, without ever bending yourself or forgetting who you are. To inspire change is to realize that your target audience must know you as much as you know them. My goal is to always be working toward inspiring something or someone, because that will mean I am always learning, accepting, and loving.

Inspiring a new foundation:

A New 20/20 Vision is a call to action for everyone. We are called to create a world in which our love for one another will outshine our misunderstanding. We are called to create a world filled with compassion. We are called to lay the very foundation our children will stand on—a world in which we will have to teach our grandkids about inequality—explaining it in detail—because it will be too unimaginable for them to truly grasp.

Now is the time to inspire by being inspired. Now is the time to be a person who doesn't turn a blind eye to injustice. Now is the time to be a person who promotes togetherness and positivity in all circumstances. People are watching you and learning from you.

How much effort are you willing to give, in order to create a life that brings you happiness?

How will you use your voice and your action to inspire others?

How will your story affect the change you desire to make?

It's one thing to inspire, it's a whole other thing to inspire inspiration.

CONCLUSION

Equipped with our New 20/20 Vision, we can finally see our path with clarity.

With our New 20/20 Vision, we can find whatever path we seek because we are dedicated to the journey, and we have reprogrammed our goals. We have the ability to define the moments in our lives, without letting those moments define us.

We smile, knowing that sometimes happiness is just giving yourself permission to explore what makes you happy. We laugh constantly, even at ourselves, for we know laughter has the ability to cure the soul and warm the heart.

We celebrate diversity in thought, words, and ideologies, using each day and each interaction to grow in our appreciation and understanding of the world and all the people in it.

We quiet the noise of negative external influences, in order to share our authentic selves with the world, rooted in positivity and a constant perspective of thankfulness.

We positively filter all the messages that come our way, knowing that our mind can create the world we desire. We turn communication into purposeful action, finding joy and happiness in the "now."

We remember what we bring to the table, feeling empowered in who we are and the effort and passion we bring to all the things we do.

If we're living, we're loving. To love is to believe in an optimistic hope and kindness toward ourselves and the incredible possibilities of a brighter world—a place where one person has the ability to make a difference.

With our New 20/20 Vision, we can break away from the restraints we put ourselves in, as well as the restraints others put on us. We take the high road, no matter the circumstance, inspiring those who look up to us for inspiration. We are focused and aligned with whom, and what, we invest our time and effort, knowing life's true costs.

With our New 20/20 Vision, we live out the change we desire for the world by making each day one to remember. So ask yourself this question; will you remember *today* in ten years? Make today unforgettable. 2020 is over, and it's time to feel alive again.

You have your new vision, and the time is now. You can't go back to the way things used to be. You're free. Your mind is clear. You know there is a better path. Liberate your authentic self and take your first step into your new life, your new journey. Unlock your mind and heart, to discover your new vision. **Welcome to the first day of the rest of your life.**

INDEX

Intro

Rooted in happiness
6 ways to create sustainable happiness........... 4

Finding your authentic self 7
Communication 17
5 key areas of communication 18
Positive soul communication...................... 19
Listening...................................... 25
It's not all about you 28
Be a thought provider/ thought provoked... 29
Positive filtering.............................. 30
Speak with purpose 37
Tolerance and understanding 38
Highlight happiness.............................. 39
Speak positivity into existence..................... 40
Don't give bad advice................................... 41
Complaining 42
"Ya....But..." 44
Finding the perfect in imperfection 45
Saying sorry................................... 48
File your engine not the fire 49
Communication and relationships.............. 51
Highlight strengths................................... 55
Affirmation 56
Give voice to what can be done 57
Love and affirmation................................ 58

Challenge one another 59
Intentions 59
Cut the blame.............................. 61
Comparing 62
Bottle identity 62
Take 10.. 63
Avoid blockers 64
Find your moments 65
Be authentic 67

Reprogramming
Morning intake 71
Adversity 73
Sacrifice...................................... 76
Darkness and pain 76
Bad moods.................................... 79
"I'm tired".................................... 80
Holes from the past 83
Judgment / insecurity.............. 83
Jealousy / envy 84
Hate / ignorance 85
Insecurity.................................... 87
Stress.. 87
Fear of the unknown 88
Dreams 89
Make a plan 90
Decision making............................ 90
Time.. 91

Work 92
Chaos 93
Ownership 94
Possessions 97
Perspective 98
Anticipation 99
Winning and losing 101
Confidence 104
Value 106
First looks / beauty 108
Type 109
Identity 110
Perfection 110
Appreciation 111
Scope 113
Forgiveness 114
Thankfulness 114
4th quarter 117
Expectations 118
Obligations 120
Non believers 121
Truth 121
Preference 124
Small talk 124
Can't to Can 125
Group happiness 126
Bedtime intake 127
Future happiness 127

Daily applications
Start small 132
Positive addictions 132
Courage 133
Add time / create lists 134
Silence the ring 135
Find your moment 136
Excel in your 95% 137
Find a first 138
Start a streak 139

Happiness on display 139
Daily gambler 140
Eliminate frustrations 142
Fight fear 143
Take the trash out 144
Chart towards happiness / stressors 145
Define yourself 147
Saturday morning 149
Eliminate excuses 149
Constant perspective 150
I get to ! 150
Today is special 151
Improve a hat 151
Transitions 152
Live in the journey 152
Puzzle pieces 153
Sorry into action 154
Future starts today 154
Find what your looking for 155
One step at a time 156
Make adjustments 157
Adds percent 158
Smile 158
Change perception 159
Be thankful 160
Mantras 161
Start today 162

Happiest you
Scouting report 169
Happiness in stages 172
The little things 173

Inspire inspiration
Organic inspiration 180
Find what inspires you 180
New foundation 182

Conclusion

ABOUT THE AUTHOR

Taylor Rochestie is a professional athlete who's traveled the world playing basketball for over 11 years. Having lived in 12 countries, immersing himself in local cultures and learning about the diversity of life's "truths." He offers a unique perspective, by sharing his New 20/20 Vision for the future. Using a positive filter to all that he encounters, Taylor is unwavering in optimism and powered with a purposeful voice to inspire positivity and happiness. Taylor is also an author, speaker, husband and father who is currently overseas playing professional basketball.

Made in the USA
Las Vegas, NV
21 February 2021

18303448R00115